The Bar/Bat Mitzvah Survival Guide

The Bar/Bat Mitzvah Survival Guide

by Randi Reisfeld

A Citadel Press Book
Published by Carol Publishing Group

A Citadel Press Book
Published by Carol Publishing Group
Citadel Press is a registered trademark of Carol Communications, Inc.

Editorial offices: 600 Madison Avenue, New York, N.Y. 10022
Sales & Distribution Offices: 120 Enterprise Avenue, Secaucus, N.J. 07094

In Canada: Canadian Manda Group, P.O. Box 920, Station U, Toronto, Ontario M8Z 5P9

Queries regarding rights and permissions should be addressed to Carol Publishing Group, 600 Madison Avenue, New York, N.Y. 10022

Carol Publishing Group books are available at special discounts for bulk purchases, for sales promotions, fund raising, or educational purposes. Special editions can be created to specifications. For details, contact: Special Sales Department, Carol Publishing Group, 120 Enterprise Avenue, Secaucus, N.J. 07094.

Manufactured in the United States of America

10 9 8 7 6 5 4 3 2 1

Library of Congress Cataloging-in-Publication Data

Reisfeld, Randi.
    The bar/bat mitzvah survival guide / by Randi Reisfeld.
        p.   cm.
    "A Citadel Press book."
    ISBN 0-8065-1295-4
    1. Bar mitzvah etiquette. 2. Bat mitzvah etiquette. I. Title.
    BJ2078.B3R45   1992
    395'.24—dc20   92-4884
                                                      CIP

This book is dedicated to the memories of
Sidney Hoffman and Maurice Reisfeld,
my children's grandfathers.

Acknowledgments

For sharing their expertise, knowledge, and opinions the author sincerely thanks

Rabbi H. Philip Berkowitz and Cantor Miranda Kark Beckenstein of Temple Beth Or, Washington Township, New Jersey.

For sharing their experiences and memories, and for being supportive, the author sincerely thanks

Sandy and Rich Alpern, Passi Bayewitz, Karen and Paul Berchman, Sandy Choron, Cheryl Dauber, Eileen and Fred Eichler, Susan and Saul Gardner, Bob Gilbert, Alice and Norman Goldberg, Estelle Hoffman, Joyce and Howard Jaffe, Sharyn and Michael Kail, Jane and Denis Kalfus, Gay and Gene Kassan, Diane and Russell Klein, Bea Langerman, Sandy and Duffy Lautz, Alice and Bruce Lee, Laura and Michael Mandelbaum, Barbara and Melissa Poser, Regina Reisfeld, Fay Weinstein—and all their children, without whom they probably wouldn't have many Bar/Bat Mitzvah experiences or memories!

For making this book a reality, the author wishes to thank

Stacey Woolf of Bob Woolf Associates and Hillel Black of Carol Publishing.

And because without them, there would have been no inspiration for this book, the author lovingly thanks

Marvin, Scott, and Stefanie Reisfeld.

Author to Reader

Soon after my son was born, or so it seems, I began hearing it: an off-the-cuff comment here (from a relative, usually), "Just think, in a few years we'll have a Bar Mitzvah!" an only half-joking question there (from a friend, usually), "So, have you started saving for the Bar Mitzvah yet?"

Knee deep in baby diapers and colic, it was hard for me to think beyond toilet training and sleeping through the night—although I admit I did use to imagine Scott as the first Bar Mitzvah boy still in diapers. But in general, I mostly ignored the references to an event that seemed so far away. In those days, "BM" meant only one thing, and it wasn't Bar Mitzvah!

Looking back, however, maybe I should have paid some attention.

For although toddlerhood *is* a ridiculously early time to start thinking about it, the years do go by awfully quickly. Before I knew it, we were checking out temples, religious schools, and car pools to Hebrew school; on the road, actually, by fourth grade, to Scott's Bar Mitzvah.

For us, it turned out to be a road untraveled by anyone we knew well—of our friends and relatives, we were the first. In this journey we were on our own, but for the dim and distant memory of my husband's Bar Mitzvah. And, we figured, times must have changed a lot since then.

What we found out was that only in some ways had they changed; in others, they hadn't at all. We had a lot to learn.

Putting it all together from scratch, to have the kind of celebration that expressed our love for and pride in our son, mixing tradition with our own creativity and making it all fit into our not-so-deep pocketbook, was a challenge.

To say the least.

Keeping our sanity through it all was a bigger one.

But put it all together we did. In the end, we had one of the best days of our lives together as a family and with our extended family of friends.

It would have been a lot easier and a lot less frustrating, however, had I known then what I know now. This book is all about what I know now.

Contents

Chapter One

The Bar/Bat Mitzvah Service

"Today I am a man."

When I was growing up in the 1950s, we were told that becoming a Bar Mitzvah meant that you were now an adult. Since no distinction was made between the literal and the symbolic, or the secular or religious significance of that statement, no one really believed it. And no one really believes it now. Indeed, no one in his right mind could look at the *pitsela* with the pimples at the pulpit—standing on a milk crate so he can even see the Torah—and think, "This is an adult." *This* is not an adult—*this* (in his secular life, at least) is more like a hormone with running shoes, about to take a flying leap into the great abyss we call adolescence (oy vay, but that's another book).

However, in his or her religious life, becoming a Bar or Bat Mitzvah really does symbolize a particular and very significant coming of age, an entry into the Jewish community. No one is saying that our thirteen-year-olds are ready for real man- or womanhood; but they are ready at that age to *start* being responsible in one aspect of their lives.

Becoming a Bar/Bat Mitzvah means that a child is now responsible for fulfilling *mitzvot*—which can mean commandments, or good deeds—and is accountable for his or her sins. It means the parents can shed their religious responsibility for the child (Orthodox men recite the blessing: "Blessed are You, Lord our God, King of the Universe, who has released me from the burden of this child"). It means, among other things, the Bar Mitzvah can now be counted as a member of a *minyan*, or quorum for prayer; can wear a *tallit*, or prayer shawl; and is eligible for an *aliyah* (see the next chapter) and responsible for following the teachings of the Torah, such as giving to *tzedakah* (charity) and fasting on Yom Kippur, the Day of Atonement. Traditionally, for boys, this happens at thirteen years and one day. In the first century C.E., ancient rabbis decided that this is the age when one begins to reason soundly, exhibit good judgment, and control one's desires (obviously, the ancient rabbis hadn't met my son). When Bat Mitzvahs came into being—they were started in 1922 as a parallel ceremony by Rabbi Mordecai Kaplan, the founder of the Reconstructionist movement (whose oldest daughter, Judith, was the first Bat Mitzvah)—the age chosen was twelve. Even then they knew that girls mature more quickly.

What's interesting, however, is that according to strict interpretation of Jewish law, becoming a Bar/Bat Mitzvah happens automatically—with or without pomp, circumstance, or ceremony!

Usually, however, a child's reaching religious majority is publicly acknowledged. It is done by calling the child up to the *bimah* or pulpit (*aliyah* actually means to go up) to stand before the Torah and accept his or her new responsibilities as a Jew. Depending on the tradition at your temple, this is done in a variety of ways.

In some synagogues, the Bar/Bat Mitzvah may lead the congregation in prayer, may recite special prayers chosen for the day, and/or may recite the blessings before and after a portion of the Torah is read. In others, the Bar/Bat Mitzvah not only recites the blessings, but reads the entire portion (*parasha*) of that week. In still others, he/she is responsible for just the final section of that week's reading, which is called the *maftir*.

In addition, he/she may recite the *haftarah*—readings from the Prophets which complement that week's Torah reading. In yet other congregations, the Bar/Bat Mitzvah is allowed to deliver a *d'var Torah,* which is a "learned commentary" on the portion that has just been read, to show he/she has mastered some aspect of Jewish learning.

Traditions and philosophies differ, but the concept remains the same: after years of study, the Bar/Bat Mitzvah can now stand before the congregation, accept the responsibilities of the religion, and show he/she is literate. He or she may now be able to lead a service, read Hebrew, read from the Torah, chant the haftarah.

This is a beginning, a basis from which to practice and learn about Judaism. It is a declaration that our children know something about their history, their religion, and their spirituality. It is an invitation into Jewish adulthood, and into the Jewish community. What actually happens during the Bar or Bat Mitzvah service differs according to each individual temple, and you should be completely aware of the traditions of your temple well before your child's big day. Those differences range from when the service takes place, to the extent of the Bar/Bat Mitzvah's participation, to the way in which you as a parent may participate.

Some of these variations can be quite extraordinary—and often have nothing to do with whether the synagogue is Orthodox, Conservative, Reconstructionist, Reform, or any of the Sephardic sects. For within each one of those, you will find differences in the way the Bar/Bat Mitzvah service is conducted.

If you or your spouse have strong feelings about what *must* occur during the service (for example, the child must read from the Torah), then you really ought to know what the temple's traditions are about the Bar/Bat Mitzvah's responsibilities before you affiliate yourself. After your child has prepared for four years is not the time to find that because she is a girl, her Bat Mitzvah must be held on a Sunday—and there *is* no Torah service on most Sundays. That is the policy at a Conservative synagogue I know of; yet in a nearby Orthodox one, girls read from the Torah, do the blessings, and chant a haftarah too. (Of course, no women are allowed aliyot in that temple, and are traditionally seated apart from the men.)

So look before you leap.

In some congregations, you may choose the date your child becomes a Bar/Bat Mitzvah; some offer the choice of any day the Torah is read: Mondays, Thursdays, Rosh Hodesh (the beginning of the Hebrew month), the Sabbath, or holidays. In others, you have no choice: Bar and Bat Mitzvah services are held only on specific days. In some, the boys have the choice; the girls do not. In one synagogue, girls may only become a Bat Mitzvah on Friday nights; in another, only on Sundays—and only in the spring.

If you're in a place where you have a choice of synagogues, it's easy and advisable to check around first and find out these details. Many people, however, don't have such wide-ranging choices and must go along with the nearby synagogue's policy, whatever it is.

Still, you should know the confines before you begin the Bar/Bat Mitzvah process: the fewer surprises you are dealt about the big day, the better.

Your Part in the Ceremony

The extent of parental participation is another thing that differs dramatically from temple to temple. In some, you ascend the bimah and play an integral role in the service; in others, you sit in your seat and never open your mouth. In still others, only the father gets to participate while the mother beams proudly—albeit silently—from her seat. The benefits of maximum participation in your child's Bar/Bat Mitzvah service are bountiful and long-lasting. In other words: do as much as you can.

Here's a hot flash: few parents participating in their *first* child's Bar/Bat Mitzvah are truly prepared for the emotional wallop it packs. Often you've spent so much time on the details of the party, you don't even think about how you're going to feel watching "the light of your life" stand before everyone you know and recite the prayers, blessings, Torah portion, and haftarah. You see the concrete evidence of what your child has accomplished, how he or she has grown. The pride, the love, the joy, are unconditional—and completely overwhelming. Grown men have been known to burst into tears watching their child becoming a Bar or Bat Mitzvah. But there's no reason to be embarrassed. Pride in and love for your offspring are pure and basic human emotions. (Goodness knows, when they become full-fledged teenagers you'll cry again—and it won't be out of pride.)

It's not only out of love for your child that you will find yourself so overwhelmed with emotion, however. When it hits you that not only is *your* child up there today, chanting a particular Torah portion, but in synagogues all over the world, other Jewish children are becoming Bar/Bat Mitzvah at that very moment, reciting from the same *sidra* (portion) of our Torah, there is a feeling of connectedness to our people that is absolutely chilling.

So if you have the opportunity, absolutely accept an aliyah (it will be explained in Chapter 2) or, at the very least, an honor on that day. In some temples you are allowed to recite a parent's prayer to your child, in front of the congregation. It may be hard to articulate the things you want to say to your son or daughter at that moment, but if you've thought it through, written it out first (and gone over it with the rabbi), it can add significantly to the moment.

Many temples go even further and allow the parents to actually make a speech. In some, the talks are Torah-driven, commenting on and drawing parallels between the portion that's been read and something significant about the child, or the family. Other speeches, however, are solely about the Bar/Bat Mitzvah. I have heard speeches that seemed to go on forever, starting with "How beautiful you were in your Pampers," and others that were so moving, they touched the heart and soul of every guest in attendance.

While I really don't think long-winded speeches detailing every moment of the child's life ("Oh, and I remember when you came home with your first report card") are particularly appropriate (especially if you're sharing the Bar/Bat Mitzvah with another family), I do think a moving reminder of what the day is all about, and perhaps a brief tribute to the family, friends, and congregants who are there to share it with you, does much to add to the meaningfulness of the ceremony. In years to come, hopefully your child will remember what you said that day, and perhaps it will be a source of strength when it is needed.

Even if your temple allows no overt participation, you can still—and probably should—become involved in the preparation. Especially if you didn't have a Jewish education yourself, take the opportunity to learn along with your child. (Okay, this assumes the child's willingness to share the experience with you. On some level at least, most will.)

Ask questions of the rabbi, the cantor, the temple's educational leader: What prayers will be recited at my child's ceremony? What is their significance? What is my child's Torah portion, what is it about? What exactly is a haftarah and how is it decided which part my child will chant? Why does he/she chant anyway?

Some temples, responding to a need among the congregation, offer a crash course in Bar/Bat Mitzvah preparations for the parents. If your temple doesn't, perhaps you could suggest it. You may be surprised to find out that many people would love to take such a course—or even just a class or two—but were embarrassed to admit their ignorance.

Asking questions along with attending Bar/Bat Mitzvah services at your own temple is the best way to familiarize yourself with the process. You don't have to be invited to attend a Bar/Bat Mitzvah service, especially when they are held on Shabbat. The temple is always open to the community and, frankly, it behooves you to attend services. You will feel a lot more comfortable if you know what's going on—and why.

Naturally, all this is time-consuming and demands a major

commitment. And how many of us really have the time? The answer is simple: you do have the time and energy (you will find it somehow) to devote to the party that will take place afterward. If you want to send a message to your child that the service is the significant part of the occasion, then you must also find the time and energy to devote to that portion of his or her special day. It's one way to let your child know that his/her Bar/Bat Mitzvah is more than just a big party.

Preparation goes a long way toward alleviating fear—yours *and* your child's. Rabbis have seen parents so nervous about their child's Bar/Bat Mitzvahs, they've been on tranquilizers (the parents, that is—though probably some of the rabbis considered it too). Parents are most nervous about the same things that terrify their children, the what-ifs: "What if I goof up? What if I fall down? What if I laugh? What if I cry? What if I blank out, forget everything I've ever learned, what if I mispronounce the Hebrew? And all in front of everyone I know—my relatives and, worse, my friends?

Helping your child cope is part of helping him/her prepare. And that is one of the most important things you *can* do, whether or not you ever go up on the bimah. Reassuring your child (and yourself) that no matter what happens on that day you will always love and be proud of him/her, may go a long way toward chasing away the what-if monster. What seems to have helped calm most of the kids I know is saying, "It doesn't matter if you goof, because no one will notice anyway." (This, of course, assumes you're in a temple where the rabbi and cantor are understanding. And it's always helpful if your rabbi and/or cantor are near the child, there to prompt if the need arises.)

You can also say, "If so-and-so"—pick the goofiest kid you know—"can do it, so can you." And, of course, the most important of all: "It doesn't matter because everyone is here to share this day with you, to celebrate your Bar/Bat Mitzvah *and* your birthday. Everyone is here because they love you. And when you love someone, you don't care if they made a mistake reading Hebrew."

You can help by listening as he chants his Torah portion, as she recites her haftarah. Encourage them to practice out loud. Offer to help (but don't *do* it) with the *d'var Torah,* the commentary on the portion.

To pressure your child into a perfect performance is to ask for trouble. That's when the what-ifs become reality (one Bar Mitzvah boy was so unnerved, he threw up on the bimah). Above all, remember that, contrary to the religious significance of his or her age, this is a child. Don't expect the wisdom and polish of an adult. The Bar Mitzvah is not a performance, it's part of a worship service, and the kid is doing the best he/she can.

Making It Meaningful

The ceremony itself is meaningful, touching, chilling, and a personal memory you will have forever, without the benefit, even, of photographs or video recordings. But still, you may want to add other layers.

Many people have taken the opportunity of their child's Bar/Bat Mitzvah to express their beliefs and values—and once again to remind everyone of the spiritual significance of the day. As one rabbi said, "to put the emphasis on the Mitzvah, instead of the Bar."

Here are several ways of doing just that.

If the temple allows it, and with your child:

- *Attend services and rehearsals.* Don't just leave the child there alone. Learn along with him or her.
- *Write your own ceremony.* This takes a lot of advance planning and work, and certainly you would need to work with your spiritual leaders, but it can be the most fulfilling and meaningful way of conducting a Bar/Bat Mitzvah.
- *Choose a special prayer,* poem, or piece of music, one that has personal significance for your family, and ask for it to be included in the service. Then have it printed up for guests to recite along with the child.
- *Compose a "parents prayer."* If this is not something com-

monly done at your temple, find out if there is some way of instituting it. If your child's service is held during a regular Shabbat service, keeping your thoughts in prayer form is more appropriate than stopping the service to inject your speech into it.

- *Choose a date with special significance,* if you can do so. Review Torah portions and see if you can come up with one that holds personal meaning for your child, such as one that was read many years ago by a favorite relative. Or pick a holiday on which to have the Bar/Bat Mitzvah. You may get more aliyot and perhaps you can conceptualize and draw a theme around that holiday for the party. If it's during Pesach (Passover), the theme can be springtime; if it's Hanukkah, you can put menorahs at each table and have each table light a candle.
- *Reintroduce the custom of pelting the Bar/Bat Mitzvah with candy,* as some families have done, to signify the sweetness of the day. It's doubtful you'll get any flack about that one from your child!
- *Passing the Torah from generation to generation* is a beautiful and symbolic portion of many services. If it is done in your synagogue, be sure to participate with grandparents and great-grandparents if possible.

And here are some things you can do regardless of your temple's practices:

- *Study together.* Find appropriate books on the subject, and talk about the significance of the upcoming event in your child's life.
- *Create a family tree* with your child, so they can see the continuity of the generations, and how they are a link in the chain.
- *Give your child a family heirloom to use on that day:* a relative's tallit, a grandmother's prayerbook, a favorite uncle's Torah commentary.
- *Draw a parallel between something in the child's Torah portion*

and something personally appropriate that brings the meaning home. My daughter's portion talked about Jews leaving their homeland in order to attain their freedom, starting all over in a foreign land—often in much more primitive circumstances than the ones they left. I pointed out that the Russian Jews in our town who are pumping gas and cleaning other people's houses were professionals—engineers and accountants in their homeland—but had to give that up in order to start a new life and enjoy freedom in another country.

- *Do a mitzvah project* together with your child, some kind of community service.
- *Arrange to donate a portion of the Bar/Bat Mitzvah gifts* to charity. Let the child decide on the charity. For an adult Jew, tzedakah (giving to charity) is an obligation, not a choice: now that your child is becoming an adult Jew, this is an important, doable responsibility he or she can fulfill.

One of the most touching gestures I have seen at a Bat Mitzvah was the note tucked into the invitation my daughter received a while back. The note was from the Bat Mitzvah girl and it said, in part: "Dear Family & Friends, I want to help the homeless and needy people in my area. One way for you to help me is to bring nonperishible food items to my temple on the day of my Bat Mitzvah.... If everyone brings a few things, many people will benefit." This is a child who was truly ready to become a Bat Mitzvah—to accept her responsibilities and to remember those less fortunate on "her day." Did she go on to have a big, splashy party afterward? You bet. Was the meaning of the day lost in the "excess" of the party. No way.

Ultimately, of course, what brings the most meaning of all to your child's Bar/Bat Mitzvah is that he or she has reached a pinnacle of life, and that you have tried to bring together all those who love him or her, to share it with you. I can't think of anything more moving and meaningful than that.

The Torah—A Beginner's Guide

The essence of the Bar/Bat Mitzvah is that your child comes up to the bimah in the presence of the Torah. He or she may read from it, recite the blessings before and after a portion is read, or simply be there while it is opened and read. Whatever your temple allows, the Torah is central to your child's becoming a Bar/Bat Mitzvah.

If you are like me and didn't know, here's what it is: The Torah is the Jewish constitution, God's will as understood by human beings, containing the laws by which we live. It is concerned with every aspect of how we live. The written portion is on a scroll; the oral interpretation defines the written and is called the Talmud.

The Torah is the first five volumes of the Bible (also called the Five Books of Moses): Genesis, Exodus, Leviticus, Numbers, and Deuteronomy. The Torah is divided into fifty-four portions (called parashas or sidras) and one or two are read each week in an annual cycle (though a few temples use a triennial cycle). Each parasha is further divided into seven parts, each called an aliyah.

It is entirely possible that children whose Bar/Bat Mitzvahs are in the same week—regardless of the year—will have the same Torah portion to read.

Questions You Should Ask

Ideally, you should have the answers to these questions before you join a temple. In reality, we choose our temples for a variety of reasons, the least of which is their Bar or Bat Mitzvah policies. However, it's a good idea to know these things before you start planning.

The ones to ask are your rabbi, the cantor, the principal of the religious school, the Bar/Bat Mitzvah chairperson (if one exists), and, most important, parents in the temple who have gone through it.

1. What are the exact requirements my child has to meet in order to become a Bar/Bat Mitzvah? How many years of Hebrew school must be completed?

2. What else will be asked of the child? Many temples require some kind of community service, or attendance at a specific number of worship services, or participating in other Bar/Bat Mitzvahs that same year.

3. What actually happens at the service? Okay, you may feel dumb asking this question, and the answer will be provided by going to services. But even when I went, I didn't understand what was going on: it helps to ask *and* to write it down (First, the morning prayers are said, then we start the Torah service. When the Torah is lifted, we have the passing down of the Torah from generation to generation ceremony, and so forth). Knowing what was coming when can be very helpful.

4. What are the traditions in this temple during the Bar/Bat Mitzvah service?

5. What is the temple's philosophy regarding the service?

6. Do we have our choice of dates, days of the week, or times?

7. Will our child's ceremony be in tandem with another child's? (In many synagogues, the congregation is so large that two children must share the day.) If so, what parts of the service will we be sharing and which will we do alone?

8. How long is the service and what time does it start?

9. What part can we as parents play in it?

10. How many aliyot will be allotted on that day?

11. May we audio or videotape the service?

12. Is there a special Bar/Bat Mitzvah fee? How much is it and when does it have to be paid?

Chapter Two

Aliyot and Honors

The most heartwarming story I ever heard about aliyot and honors was the Bar Mitzvah where nearly every one of the guests participated. They came forward in clusters according to their relationship to the Bar Mitzvah boy—all his first cousins, all his second cousins, and so forth—and either recited the Torah blessings or were honored by being allowed to lift and dress the Torah scroll, or open and close the ark in which it is kept. The rabbi heartily welcomed them all up to the bimah. He was thrilled at the overall audience participation, and so were the boy and his parents.

The most heartwrenching story I ever heard about honors and aliyot was the one where the family only had a prescribed number to give out and chose to bestow them on the father's first cousins. Except there was one cousin too many, so one person in that group didn't get an aliyah. Right in the middle of the Torah service, he and his entire family walked out—and haven't spoken to the Bar Mitzvah boy or his family since.

Clearly, assigning aliyot and honors can be a highly charged undertaking. It can add immeasurably to the joyous feelings of the day, or can ruin it. Most people's experiences fall somewhere in between.

What They Are

The word *aliyot* is pronounced al-lee-YOHT, and it is the plural of *aliyah*. One person is assigned one aliyah; the family of the Bar Mitzvah may get to assign several aliyot. It means "to

29

ascend," and within the context of the Bar/Bat Mitzvah it means to come up to the Torah and recite the blessings (*b'rachot*) before and after a section of the Torah is read. The blessings are exactly the same each time. If seven people come up and recite the blessings, they are saying the same exact words. The blessings are not mysterious or particularly difficult to master, even for a novice. Basically, you are giving testimony to God and to the Jewish people.

An *honor* differs from an aliyah in that it's a nonspeaking role. The person who is chosen to be honored participates in the service by typically opening and closing the ark, and/or lifting and dressing the Torah after it is removed from the ark, or upon its return to the ark.

Both honors and aliyot are related to the Torah ceremony and take place during that part of the service.

The number of aliyot and honors depends upon the tradition at your temple and on the day of the week (and time of day) your Bar Mitzvah service is held. Often, however, at a Saturday morning service, there are seven aliyot (be aware, however, that the seventh is often reserved for the Bar/Bat Mitzvah child). On all other days, there are fewer.

Clearly, what you need to do first, before starting to think about the people you want to honor, is find out exactly what the policy is in your temple. Ask either the rabbi or cantor:

1. How many aliyot will I be allowed to assign?
2. What are the restrictions in terms of whom I may ask? (In many temples, only Jews are allowed an aliyah or an honor and only those who are past Bar/Bat Mitzvah age.)
3. Are women allowed an aliyah or honor? (In many Orthodox congregations, the answer is No.)
4. Is there a difference in restrictions between honors and aliyot? In some temples you don't have to be Jewish or of Bar Mitzvah age in order to open or close the ark (an honor).

5. Is there an option to say the blessings in English?
6. May more than one person come up and recite the blessings together?
7. Will the Hebrew or transliteration or English translation of the blessings be posted on the lectern next to the Torah?
8. Must I chose someone from a specific hereditary clan (Kohen) for the first aliyah, and someone from another tribe (Levite) for the second?
9. Will the men I ask have to wear tallitot and/or *kippot* (yarmulkes)?
10. Is there some kind of dress restriction for the women who come up?
11. Will I have to submit a list of the Hebrew names of those I choose to honor?
12. How will the people be summoned up to the bimah? Will they be called by their Hebrew names, English names, or will I have to instruct them exactly when to go up?

In addition to getting the answers to these questions, I heartily recommend going to other Bar/Bat Mitzvah services *at your temple*. (Remember, you don't have to be invited and you shouldn't feel awkward in the least about being there. A temple is a place of worship, open to everyone.) Pay close attention to the Torah service and see how other people handle aliyot and honors. You will also get a feel for how the rabbi and cantor respond toward the people who come up. Some clergy exude warmth, are tolerant of mispronunciations, and make people feel comfortable; others clearly are more rigid and absolutely intolerant—I actually heard one member of the clergy describe it this way— of "people who butcher the b'rachot." That is not exactly conducive to feeling comfortable on the bimah.

The more you know, the better feel you'll have for how your guests will be received during the ceremony—and the easier it will be to choose the people you want to honor.

Making the Choices

Actually, it's never easy to make this choice. In some cases, it's easier than others; the choices fall naturally into place and no one's feelings are hurt. In other cases (say mine, for instance) you will absolutely agonize about whom to call up. In the worst case (as happened to a friend of mine, and as described earlier in the chapter), feelings will be hurt to the point where an entire relationship is shattered. By the way, I would not place blame on the Bar Mitzvah family. They did it the best way they knew how; they didn't set out to insult anyone. It's a pity that their cousins couldn't see it that way.

So, how do you make this choice? There are no hard and fast rules except one: Don't give in to pressure from others, that is, your own parents or in-laws who will, given half the chance, start badgering you: "How can you possibly slight Aunt Hilda? She must have an honor." To which you answer: "Come and share the *simcha* (joyous event), but don't try to manage it."

First, you sit down with your spouse or co-planner and list the possible choices. If you are divorced, this is still a major issue you need to talk about. Relatives and/or friends from all sides should be considered. (At this point, however, I wouldn't involve the Bar/Bat Mitzvah child, these choices aren't necessarily his or hers to make. Whether Great-uncle Irving should come up and recite the blessings is not an appropriate decision to be made by a thirteen-year-old.)

Honestly, the fewer aliyot and honors you have to dispose, the easier it's going to be. If you only have three, there's less chance of offending a great many people. Grandparents usually come first and everyone understands that.

If you have as many as fourteen combined aliyot and honors (as we did), the choices become trickier. Should you ask this friend, but not that one? This cousin, but not that uncle?

Many people solve the problem by choosing people in categories, that is, only the grandparents, uncles, and aunts; only the first cousins; only the immediate family; or only friends. Some people aren't that strict about the categories and decide to choose only people who have a relationship with the Bar/Bat Mitzvah. So while Great-uncle Henry, who has never actually met the child but is closely related biologically, doesn't get an aliyah, your best friend does because she has put thousands of miles on her odometer car-pooling this child.

Whatever method you use, it's a good idea to ask your choices first whether they would like an aliyah or an honor. The first time around, with our son's Bar Mitzvah, we didn't. It was a mistake. We were fairly arbitrary about the whole deal: we said, in effect, "You're the grandmother, you're the uncle, you're the aunt, you're doing it." Not that it didn't work out, but in truth most of the people we asked didn't really want to be there. They felt awkward, uncomfortable, and even embarrassed. What they did not feel was honored.

The second time we did it differently. We asked first. We explained that although we would love to honor them during our daughter's Bat Mitzvah, we would understand if they felt uncomfortable. It's okay to pass. What we ended up with was a mixed bag—one grandmother, no uncles or aunts, two of our friends, one sibling, and ourselves. The result was that the people who recited the blessings were the ones to whom it meant the most: they cared passionately about being there and felt truly honored to be part of the service. The other grandmother, uncles, aunts, and cousins had nonspeaking roles. They opened and closed the ark, lifted and dressed the Torah; they felt comfortable and honored at the same time.

Were there people we left out? Yes. Did we hurt their feelings? I hope not. If we did, I have faith that they understand that we did our best.

No matter whom you choose, you should definitely prepare people ahead of time. Everyone is nervous—especially those not familiar with Hebrew. No one wants to be surprised on that day, and everyone's afraid of looking silly. They should be instructed not only on when to come up (you might even suggest that they sit on the aisle so they can get out easily) but whom they will be following and exactly what they are supposed to do.

Some temples are very helpful and give you cue cards to distribute that say, "We are pleased you are participating in (so and so's) service. When the rabbi instructs the congregation to turn to page 417 in the prayerbook, please come up and stand next to the cantor," etc. These cards leave little to chance. If your temple does not provide them, do it yourself. Go over the service with the rabbi or cantor (if they're not receptive, ask the Bar/Bat Mitzvah chairperson, or another family who has recently been through it) and type out index cards. Don't be surprised to see people gripping their cards for dear life as they partake in the service!

I would also suggest sending a card to the aliyot people with the blessings written out: in English (if that's acceptable), in Hebrew, and in transliteration. That way, they can familiarize themselves beforehand. Older people may be rusty. Those to whom it's completely new will be grateful for the chance to learn and practice. Some families have even sent tapes of the blessing being chanted to those who will participate.

Some tips: have a pinch hitter handy, someone you're close to who knows the blessings by heart. It has happened on more than one occasion that someone you've chosen suddenly can't do it—whether because of an attack of nerves, or ill health, or tardiness getting to the temple. If you have a backup, it's one less thing for you to fret about that day (don't worry—there'll be plenty of others).

You might not want to give someone elderly or frail the honor of lifting and dressing the Torah; it's a heavy scroll.

Don't immediately eliminate friends of the Bar/Bat Mitzvah child from your list of aliyot possibilities. Especially if you don't have close relatives, it might be really special to ask your child's best friend, especially if that child has recently become a Bar/Bat Mitzvah. Those youngsters can be guaranteed to know the prayers. And that kind of memory will be especially poignant to them in later years.

When making your choices, again take into account how your guests will be received by the rabbi and cantor. At this point, you have to accept the attitudes of your clergy—and you don't want to make your guests unduly uncomfortable. So if you have a rabbi and cantor who truly feel that those who mispronounce the b'rachot and pfumfer through the prayers are showing disrespect at a sacred moment, you might not want to ask people who have rarely been inside a temple and really aren't familiar with the routine. Call them up at the candle-lighting instead (see Chapter 15). If, on the other hand, your rabbi is the kind of person who feels it's more significant to have as many people as possible participate, regardless of their fluency in Hebrew, by all means, call the whole *mishpocha* (relatives) up. It will be all the more joyous and meaningful.

One more important point: when choosing whom you will honor, don't forget yourself, especially if you belong to a temple where traditionally there are few ways for the parents to be involved in the ceremony. You and your spouse deserve this honor and often your Bar/Bat Mitzvah really wants you to have it. (Okay, so sometimes it's because "I studied hard and had to memorize my whole haftarah—show me you can do this one little part," but nevertheless, they have a point.)

If you haven't had a lot of religious training, it's natural that you may feel insecure (which is exactly how your child probably feels), but putting the effort into learning the prayers is well worth it. Not only is it another way of showing your child that the service is more significant than the party (you're taking just as much time preparing for it); but it's not that hard and you will feel proud and joyous the moment you do them (okay, the moment you finish). So get the cantor or rabbi to teach the prayers to you. Write them down in your *own* transliteration (I found it more helpful to read my own notes than a printed set). Then, walk up to the bimah with the same index card or piece of paper you've been practicing with. Or make a tape and practice with that.

Another tip: you might feel silly, but trust me, it's easier to chant it than to say it. The words fall into place more naturally.

And just as you tell your children that it really, in the long run, doesn't matter if they goof up on a word or two, remind yourself of that too. You're trying, you're doing something for your child and for yourself. Think of it this way: a little piece of your child's history will always be up on that bimah. And now, so will a little of yours.

If you want, you can start practicing now. Here are the Torah blessings in English and Hebrew, with a transliteration. They are the same blessings that are said in every temple.

Before the Torah is read:

בָּרְכוּ אֶת־יְיָ הַמְבֹרָךְ׀

בָּרוּךְ יְיָ הַמְבֹרָךְ לְעוֹלָם וָעֶד׀

בָּרוּךְ אַתָּה, יְיָ אֱלֹהֵינוּ, מֶלֶךְ הָעוֹלָם, אֲשֶׁר בָּחַר־בָּנוּ מִכָּל־
הָעַמִּים וְנָתַן־לָנוּ אֶת־תּוֹרָתוֹ. בָּרוּךְ אַתָּה, יְיָ, נוֹתֵן הַתּוֹרָה.

Ba-re-chu et A-do-nai ha-me-vo-rach!
Ba-ruch A-do-nai ha-me-vo-rach le-o-lam va-ed!
Ba-ruch a-ta, A-do-nai E-lo-hei-nu, me-lech ha-o-lam,
a-sher ba-char ba-nu mi-kol ha-a-mim, ve-na-tan la-nu et
To-ra-to.
Ba-ruch a-ta, A-do-nai, no-tein ha-to-rah.

After the Torah is read:

בָּרוּךְ אַתָּה, יְיָ אֱלֹהֵינוּ, מֶלֶךְ הָעוֹלָם, אֲשֶׁר נָתַן לָנוּ תּוֹרַת
אֱמֶת וְחַיֵּי עוֹלָם נָטַע בְּתוֹכֵנוּ. בָּרוּךְ אַתָּה, יְיָ, נוֹתֵן הַתּוֹרָה.

Ba-ruch a-ta, A-do-nai E-lo-hei-nu
me-lech ha-o-lam, a-sher na-tan la-nu To-rat e-met, ve-
cha-yei o-lam na-ta be-to-chei-nu.
Ba-ruch a-ta, A-do-nai, no-tein ha-to-rah.

Here's the English, which may be perfectly acceptable (and
even, in some cases, advisable):

Before:

Praise the Lord, to whom our praise is due!
Praised be the Lord, to whom our praise is due, now and
forever!
Blessed is the Lord our God, Ruler of the universe, who
has chosen us from all peoples by giving us his Torah.
Blessed is the Lord, Giver of the Torah.

After:

Blessed is the Lord our God, Ruler of the universe, who
has given us a Torah of truth, implanting within us eternal
life.
Blessed is the Lord, Giver of the Torah.

Chapter Three

But Do You Really Need a Party?

There are those who resist—recoil, even—from the very idea of making a Bar Mitzvah party. In fact, as you now know, the phrase "making a Bar Mitzvah" is a misnomer. You don't actually *make* anything; your son or daughter *becomes* a Bar/Bat Mitzvah after a prescribed amount of religious school training, at around the age of thirteen. Literally translated, the phrase means "son (daughter) of the commandments" and in the eyes of the Jewish religion, it means he or she can now be accorded full adult responsibilities and privileges as a Jew.

This in and of itself is not necessarily cause to take out a second mortgage to finance a grand hoopla. It is, however, traditionally cause to celebrate.

As far back as the fourteenth century, in Eastern Europe, the Bar (sorry, no Bats in those days) Mitzvah was a coming-of-age celebration for and by the people. Moreover, it was a community event. After the service (in those days, most often held on a Monday or Thursday, traditional days when the Torah was read), the family of the Bar Mitzvah provided, at the very least, a *kiddush* of wine and light refreshments, and more often, invited the entire community home for a large meal, to extend good wishes and blessings on the Bar Mitzvah lad.

Later, in the seventeenth and eighteenth centuries, in Western Europe, the Bar Mitzvah (still no Bats) became an even more celebratory occasion replete with a festive meal. Indeed, offering hospitality is not only traditional, but fundamental to the Jewish way of life. Sharing food after a simcha, or joyous event, came naturally to our ancestors and comes naturally to us too.

Celebration, then, is a natural extension of the Bar Mitzvah experience.

Okay, so in those days the celebration started and ended with food, blessings, and speeches—no deejays with smoke machines, face-painting clowns, or troupes of celebrity look-a-likes. But just as our ancestors celebrated in their way, we are prone to celebrate in ours.

It can be argued, then, that by having a party, you are helping to preserve an important Jewish custom, fulfilling a mitzvah, a commandment.

Still, life in America in the 1990s is a far cry from that in fourteenth-century Poland. And these days, many openly worry that our Bar Mitzvah celebrations have all but overshadowed the religious and spiritual significance of the day; the sizzle has left the steak in ashes.

"Spending a great deal of money has nothing to do with the meaning of the event," is a common refrain. Indeed, it goes on, "spending extravagantly trivializes it."

To Spend or Not to Spend

We've all heard the stories about Bar Mitzvahs that were so lavish they seemed completely contrary to the religious aspect. To most of us, renting out Giants' Stadium for 35,000 of your nearest and dearest, or chartering the *QE II*—both of which have been done—seems a little out of hand. Not to mention the well-known story about the man who thinks he is being highly original by taking the whole Bar Mitzvah party on an African safari. Suddenly they come to a complete halt. When he asks the guide why they've stopped, the guide replies: "There's another Bar Mitzvah ahead of us."

Whether that story is true or not (actually, I wouldn't doubt it), no one would argue that overspending is a legitimate concern. It is not, however, a new one. Back in the Middle Ages, rabbis argued against celebrations becoming too ostentatious and enacted laws limiting the size of the party and type of finery that could be worn. The purpose was twofold: to stave off anti-Semitic feelings about Jewish riches, and concern, even back then, that too much excess would overshadow the religious significance of the day.

The obvious response is that it doesn't have to. It is fully within your power as the parent to make sure that doesn't happen, to spend as much time and energy on making the *service* meaningful to your family, and more important, to the Bar/Bat Mitzvah child, as you do on the party. If you want your children to realize that this celebration isn't just a big party, you need to think about the meaning of it all first, and about your own responsibility.

Another point when considering the overspending argument: it's all relative. To the family of little means in Russia, what you might consider intimate and tasteful would be lavish and ridiculous, just as that safari may be to you. What's "reasonable" to you could be the price of someone else's home, or child's college education. If the person who spent $200,000 chartering the *QE II* earns millions, is that not comparable with someone else who makes $200,000 per year spending $20,000 on his child's Bar Mitzvah celebration? If that is how a zillionaire expresses herself, why is that so different from the "average, middle-class" American Jew expressing himself as best as he or she can?

The retort to that one, then, is that you're making a party not for the kids, but for the parents' friends. Even if you *can* afford to spend hundreds of thousands, should you? It's not a kids' party anymore if you do.

And what about the kids themselves? It is often then asked, when they're exposed to extravagance, don't they become jaded? And if they start these celebrations "at the top," where do you go from there? "What could you possibly do for the wedding to top this?" is another common refrain. I have even heard of youngsters comparing and critiquing the Bar Mitzvahs of their friends as if it *were* a competition.

Depending on where you live, there is also the issue of peer pressure. Even if you don't want to spend a lot of money on a gala affair, you may feel pressured into it by the community mores ("everybody does it this way") or by your own child. It's easy to dismiss this with a "Just say no" cliché, but for many of us, the reality is not so simple. We all care about the way we are perceived by others, there's no question about it. And many of us do feel trapped into spending more time and energy on the party than we really want to.

There *are* ways to fight peer pressure, but none is easy. In one community, all the children in the Bar/Bat Mitzvah class celebrated together, in one massive party, as is frequently done in Israel. In another, all the temples got together and put a ceiling on the amount each family could spend on their Bar/Bat Mitzvah celebrations. Admittedly, it was a small community and it was many years ago. It's hard to imagine that kind of pulling together in some of our larger and wealthier communities today. But perhaps it can be done on a smaller, more intimate scale. Perhaps, several years before the rounds of Bar and Bat Mitzvahs start, you can get together with a group of friends and discuss keeping all the celebrations small.

It seems, however, that the loudest and most vociferous voices against a big party are from those who (a) haven't made a Bar Mitzvah yet and aren't about to anytime soon, (b) don't have children, and (c) aren't Jewish.

To feel you have to justify what you're doing constitutes an added pressure. As long as you're doing what you need to, and what reflects you, you don't have to justify anything to anyone. Just don't invite 'em.

Finding What's Right for You

The trick is to discover what's right for you and then to do just that and no more. Find a level that you are comfortable with and then learn how much it will cost you to achieve that in your area. The form your celebration takes, from a small kiddush to a lavish black-tie affair, should be entirely up to you. And though many may choose to differ with your choice, anything is really okay as long as it reflects your family's feelings, values, and love for your child. If it turns your stomach to see so much extravagance and waste when so many in this world are hungry, scale down your own celebration and ask guests to bring something (a nonperishible donation of food) to give to an organization that feeds the hungry. One such is Mazon, which is Jewish Response to Hunger, and supports programs like soup kitchens and food pantries. Their address: 2940 Westwood Blvd., Suite 7, Los Angeles, CA 90064.

If a modest celebration doesn't satisfy your family, go for a bigger one—as long as you're not trying to outdo the next person and as long as you can afford it. No one is suggesting you go into debt or dip into the kids' college funds. Hopefully, within the pages of this book, you will find ideas on how to put together a celebration that's meaningful, tasteful, and fun, one that will satisfy your Bar/Bat Mitzvah and yourself without your having to spend more than you can afford.

Perhaps the problem is not with the big parties. Perhaps the real problem is when the kids (and their parents) view the Bar/Bat Mitzvah service as the end of the child's religious education, instead of a milestone along the way. In fact, the real oxymoron is not so much the Bar Mitzvah party, but when the child quits Hebrew school right after it. For the meaning of the event is that now—for the first time, not the last—the child may go up when the Torah is being read, and in many congregations, actually read from the Torah. The Bar/Bat Mitzvah should now be educated in how to lead a congregation in prayer, and can now be considered an adult in a religious sense.

The Bar Mitzvah is supposed to be a beginning, an entry into the Jewish community—that's what it means—not an end.

There's another overwhelming reason that we tend to celebrate the Bar Mitzvah in a big way. Life deals us all a hand of bad times and good times. And if you don't celebrate the good—rejoice in those times when your family is healthy, happy, and all together—then all you are left with are bitter memories of the bad.

The summer before my son's Bar Mitzvah, I went to four funerals, saw my mother through a difficult hospital stay, and had a megabuck car breakdown in a dangerous neighborhood. I spent a great deal of time, energy, emotional upheaval, and money on all those occasions, none of them happy ones, none of which I'd have chosen.

Does it make any less sense to spend time, energy, emotions, and money on something wonderful in your life, on an occasion when you get to bring together all the people you love? If you draw on the support of family and friends at emotionally draining times, why not celebrate with them at emotionally fulfilling ones?

I didn't come to this philosophy on my own. Years ago, I too might have joined the chorus of those who think it outrageous to make a big party. But a bittersweet experience changed my thinking forever. Several years ago, my parents and I were having a lovely dinner at an expensive restaurant. When I (in my hippie days, it should be noted) questioned the value of spending this kind of money at dinner, my father—who loved nothing more than a great meal—said, "Better to spend it here than on doctor bills." He knew whereof he spoke: he was dying. Too much time, anguish, and, yes, money had already been spent on his failing health: more was to come.

After he died, I resolved to lavish—not necessarily money, of which I never did have a lot—energy, time, and lots of emotion on the good stuff in life.

Bar and Bat Mitzvahs are part of that good stuff.

Chapter Four

Whose Bar Mitzvah Is It Anyway?

This is a key question to start with, and if you've got a ready answer, you're way ahead of the game. But the truth is that most families don't. We certainly didn't.

There's no question that you are getting ready to celebrate a major event in your child's religious and secular life, one that he or she has no doubt been preparing for, for several years.

But does that mean you leave all the decisions about the big day up to your child? Will he or she decide on everything from the guest list to the color scheme and the music to be played?

Some people go in with just this attitude, that this is a party for thirteen-year-olds, and plan a child-oriented event. Others feel that since the parents—you!—are footing the bill, they should have total control over all the particulars. And there are those intent on planning a day that grandma, grandpa, and the rest of the mishpocha, all the relatives, will *kvell* (glow with pride) over.

Most of us, however, are never completely clear about just who the "party" part is for. In fact, in most cases, there are several key players—mom, dad, grandparents, in-laws, and of course, the birthday child. And each of these players has a personal vision of just what the event will be like.

The mistake is to try to please them all. It's a mistake most of us make—the first time around, anyway.

When we first began thinking about our son's Bar Mitzvah, *I* envisioned a rather low-key brunch buffet to follow the ceremony. My mother immediately got hysterical at the thought of her relatives (most of whom I hadn't actually considered inviting, but that's another chapter) having to "stand on line." She started lobbying early on for a sit-down luncheon—so no one would have to drive home in the dark, another thought that somehow hadn't crossed my already cluttered mind. My *husband,* on another track altogether, pictured a splashy, black-tie evening event with as much razzle-dazzle as we could afford (not much, as it turned out) and lots of '60s and '70s rock 'n' roll.

We couldn't quite figure out what our *son* wanted, not right away, anyway. Because we had to make some choices about the big day quite far in advance, he really had no idea what a Bar Mitzvah was (he's one of the few Jewish boys in his school and, alas, we were the first of our friends and relatives to embark on this particular journey). So in the beginning of our planning, he had no vision.

That, of course, changed dramatically as the time drew nearer—after it was too late to make any changes. Suddenly, our little Bar Mitzvah person knew exactly what he wanted— fifty of his closest friends ("Who *are* these people?" I demanded, never having seen or heard of them in the last thirteen years); a deejay who played disco and rap music (this, of course, was after we had already hired a band); and a buffet replete with make-your-own sundaes (which I interpreted as "throw-your-own food"). To this last idea, my *daughter* (who, of course, knew exactly what she wanted five years down the road for her Bat Mitzvah) gave a rousing thumbs-ups.

We had many a blood pressure-raising argument over all of this. But you don't have to.

Compromise, clearly, is key. So are lots of advance planning and talking things through before you make any commitments.

Sitting down with your spouse (or co-planner) is really the first step and one that should be taken well in advance of your date. In fact, you may run into initial resistance ("It's two years away—who wants to even think about it now?"), but do it anyway. Finding out what the other person's ideas are—however vague—and talking through your own feelings will set the stage for less conflict later on. It also may help avoid those later "Why is this all being dumped on me?" feelings of anger and frustration. Thinking now about who will handle what responsibilities is a good idea. Perhaps you will even agree on a format for the affair. That's a major hurdle.

While I advocate engaging your husband in the early planning, I wouldn't open up the discussion to any other relatives. By this I mean: do *not* involve your own parents or in-laws. True, some will not give you a hard time about any of it and may even have some good advice. Others, however, will come to the table with a laundry list of you-musts and how-could-you-nots, such as "It *must* be kosher!" or "How could you not invite Great-aunt Sophie?" ad nauseam.

Rule of thumb number one: You can't make everyone happy. Trust me on this: you will drive yourself crazy trying to. Do it your way, do it your husband's way, do it your child's way. But to the beloved, albeit buttinsky relatives, say: "I absolutely understand how you feel and will try to accommodate you at some point. Isn't it wonderful that we're all here to share this joyous family occasion together? I love you." And then go ahead and do what you want.

It's really not as cruel and coldhearted as it sounds. The truth is, if you start trying to meet too many needs, you start fragmenting yourself and something has to give. Most often, it's the immediate family who lose out. You'll have to say to your child, "Sorry, but we can't do this because Grandma wants that," and to your husband, "Sorry, you'll have to find more money, because your mother has four hundred people she needs to invite." You start making compromises that you really shouldn't have to at this time.

This doesn't mean that you completely ignore the (usually unsolicited) input from the mishpocha. For *rule of thumb number two is:* Nobody gets hurt. As you get closer to the date, do listen and try to accommodate some of their needs. If you've picked a place for the reception that's not kosher, but one of your relatives needs a kosher meal, perhaps the caterer (if you're going that route) can provide it, without making the whole affair *glatt* (absolutely) kosher. Perhaps you *will* invite Great-aunt Sadie after all. Accommodate where you can, but not to the point where the celebration becomes their affair and not yours.

Something to remember: if the relatives—and the friends, for that matter—really love and care about you, and feel you have taken at least some of their needs into consideration, then whatever you choose to do will be fine with them.

Okay, back to planning. If you've been to other people's affairs recently, you're at an advantage. You remember what you, as a guest, liked about it and what you felt didn't work so well. You can take all that into account when planning your big day.

If, however, you're in the position we were in—we hadn't been to a Bar Mitzvah in twenty years—you will have to start from scratch. You've got to do your own research. Do it early, no matter how foolish you feel about asking availability dates of catering halls two or even three years in advance!

Part of your research, of course, is right here in this book. Exploring your options ahead of time, thinking it all through in advance, will help tremendously in the planning and executing of a smooth and joyful day.

Remember, this is supposed to be *fun* (keep reminding yourself of that), and a little ahead-of-time thought will do a lot to avoid many conflicts and headaches (unfortunately, not all of them). As you read through these pages, you'll start to get ideas on different ways to accomplish this.

While it may be relatively easy to leave your relatives out of the planning loop, obviously most Bar/Bat Mitzvahs will want some say in how the day is planned. Be advised ahead of time that you won't agree on much of it. You might think you will, but you will be disabused of that notion very quickly.

When we were planning our son's Bar Mitzvah, the extent of

his participation was nil. He went to religious school and learned his lessons; he certainly did his part in the preparation for the service. As for the party, he wanted no part of the planning. During that time, I wished for his input and dreamed happily of the day my daughter would become a Bat Mitzvah, fantasizing about all the mother-daughter fun we would have, shopping together, picking out this invitation, that dress, *bonding*. Until the time actually came, that is. That's when the fantasy fizzled. Our daughter did want to be involved, every step of the way. The planning did not exactly go according to my fantasies. Let's just say that when the time came, I longed for the days of the Bar Mitzvah, when I went my merry way, making all the decisions myself.

My daughter and I agreed on virtually nothing. What my husband and I wanted was "totally uncool" and *not* what the other kids were doing. Or it was too much *like* what the other kids were doing, and not different enough.

It's hard to say no to the light of your life. It's hard to fight the impulse to give in to every little thing he or she wants, because, after all (and here's a phrase you're going to hear often, especially from someone who's trying to sell you something), "It's *her* day." After a while, you'll start wishing for it to be the *next* day, when it's *not* her day anymore.

The lesson in all this: *controlled involvement*. Give your child lots of choices—after you've already narrowed down the field to what's acceptable. It's like when they were toddlers and insisted on dressing themselves. You didn't open up the entire field of plaids and polka dots and stripes (well, maybe *you* did), you chose four acceptable items and made that the field. Look through books of invitations first. Eliminate entire books that are too expensive and show him only those where the price fits your budget. Don't take her to the priciest teen boutique for a dress: or if you do, accept that you may end up spending megabucks. Stick with a few popular places and let her choose any dress from those stores.

With controlled involvement in mind, here are some suggestions for the "who decides what" compromises:

You and your husband (or co-planner) should have final say on:

1. The form the event takes—anything from a small, tasteful (why does tasteful always seem to come after small?) kiddush to a lavish affair, and anything in between.
2. The adult guest list.
3. Where the party will be held.
4. The main menu.
5. The kinds of music to be played, whether by a band or a deejay.
6. The photographer/video person.
7. Flowers and decorations.
8. People to be called up for the candle lighting.
9. People to be called upon for honors and aliyot.
10. Seating of the adults.

Let the child have his or her way on:

1. The invitations.
2. The color scheme.
3. The theme (if you agree there is to be one).
4. Games the band/deejay plays with the kids.
5. The kids' menu.
6. Extra entertainment (if any).
7. The favors.
8. The kids' guest list.
9. Seating of the kids.
10. His or her outfit.

You may not agree with this particular breakdown of compromises ("What if he chooses a really horrible invitation?") but it does give you something to think about.

Yes, you *are* paying and there's not a small amount of your own ego involved, and you do want your friends to have a good time. But this is the biggest day in the life of your young person, so far, and he or she deserves to have a good amount to say in the event. After all, your son or daughter will be taking center stage on the bimah and performing in front of everyone he or she and you know! That's a scary proposition all by itself.

Aside from all that, some youngsters also perceive the event as the first party they're hosting, and they're just as worried about what their friends will think and say the day after in school. That's a lot of social pressure for a just-turned-thirteen-year-old, and understanding parents can help ease the way. In more ways than one, it's the child's first step into the adult world of responsibilities and privileges, the first try at organizing a social event, where your son or daughter will be in the spotlight, taking the heat and the credit. And just as you want to be there for them as they grow in every aspect of their lives, so you will want to be as understanding and supportive as possible in this one.

So what if he chooses the world's ugliest invitation? Most people are going to trash it anyway (and you don't *have* to frame it).

Chapter Five

Money Matters

For most of us, regardless of our spirituality *or* our finances, the really big issue is: just how much this shindig is going to cost. How can we justify spending this much money and, more important, how are we going to afford it? The dollars and cents part is what causes many of us to lose our common sense; it's the root of most familial fighting, whether between husband and wife, ex husbands and wives, or parents and children. It's the rare family planning an event of this kind that escapes without at least one battle of the bucks.

We all bring a load of personal baggage to the table when we sit down to talk money. It's one of our biggest emotional button pushers. And each of us comes to it with a different mind-set. For every husband who feels this is his opportunity to prove he's "made it," there's a wife who's tearing her hair out, thinking, "This is the cost of one year of college, and we're spending it on one day!" And for every wife who must have that perfect dress, there's a husband poring over his checkbook, wondering where the money's coming from.

Part of the problem is that most of us have a fantasy about what the day is going to be like; many of us have thought about it for years. And when the fantasy goes head-to-head with the reality of our finances, we may soon find ourselves in *over* our heads. You child's Bar/Bat Mitzvah is a very emotional issue. It can be compared to looking for a house. You have an amount in mind that you want to spend, an amount that you absolutely won't, can't, refuse to go over—until you see *the* house. And fall in love with it. At that point your heart takes over and all the rationale flies out the window. You can't help yourself.

The big difference with the Bar/Bat Mitzvah is that there's always another carrot being dangled in front of your face. There's always something (more expensive than the one you had in mind) that "your child will love—her friends will go crazy— that's so perfect, how could you not buy it?"

And because this is such a sentimental event, such an emotional time, we're all vulnerable. The merchants out there know it, and prey on it. If you have an ounce of impulse in you, you're easy game. It's common to fall into the (and here's another phrase you're going to be hearing a lot of, especially from your own lips) "We're spending so much already, what's another few dollars?" syndrome. But beware: at times it's going to feel like a runaway train, especially if you don't know how and when to apply the brakes.

The way you resolve this dilemma depends on the relationship you have with your spouse (or your ex) and your child. It will be resolved pretty much the way you resolve all your other conflicts. If the relationships are basically cooperative, compromise comes more easily. If they're not, don't expect it now.

If money is one of the main buttons in your family, it really helps to go into the planning of this event with your eyes open, knowing that you're going to disagree. You must pick and choose your issues; you won't win on every point, nor will you lose every one either. The trick is finding the things you won't compromise on and being willing to give up on those you really can do without. And vice versa: know what your co-planner can't back down on, and accept it. Your child comes in later, after the major money decisions have been made.

Going into all this with your eyes open is a good idea. Figuring "we'll deal with it when the times comes" is a bad one. Here are a few tips:

Often, the temple that you join determines the course your Bar/Bat Mitzvah is going to take. So if there's still time and you don't want to spend a lot of money, it's a good idea to consider a temple where the Bar/Bat Mitzvah tradition is more low-key. If none of the families go in for outlandish affairs, there's less chance that you'll feel pressured into one.

It's a bad idea to approach this event with the idea of keeping up with, or worse, outdoing, another family. More than having the party itself, *that's* what's contradictory to the event.

It's also a bad idea to go into debt. If you have a burning need to do so, do it for the child's education, not for a Bar/Bat Mitzvah party.

It's a good idea to start saving beforehand. You've heard of Christmas clubs? Start a Bar/Bat Mitzvah club.

It's a bad idea to let other people tell you what you should and shouldn't be doing, to "do it right." Especially when their advice translates into dollars (which it usually does).

It's a good idea to hold back some money (if possible) on people from whom you're buying services—the band, the photographer, the decorator—until the party's over. That way, you've left yourself some room for negotiation if things haven't gone as you've expected.

It's also a good idea to know what your major, and less major—because there are no minor—expenses will be. In general, no matter what form the party takes, you will have four significant expenses:

1. The *place* you will be hosting the party, and the *food* you will be serving, combined, will constitute your biggest expense. Figure that 45 to 50 percent of your budget will go for this.
2. The *music/entertainment* usually comes next, accounting for about 10 percent of the total.
3. The *decorations* often account for about 10 percent also.
4. If you go in for a *photographer* and professional photo album, plus a *video* of the party, that's going to take up another 10 percent.

Which leaves 20 to 25 percent for the four million (or so it will seem) less major expenses. Some you've probably thought of, like clothing, invitations, favors, extra entertainment, and hospitality for out-of-town guests. Others you probably haven't thought of, like stamps, calligraphy, seating cards, napkins, matches, gratuities, hairdresser, kippot, food for the Oneg Shabbat, food for the "afterbirth" (see Chapter 20), food for the band, flowers for the bimah, transporting the children from the temple to the party place, and so on. Not to mention last-minute expenses like stockings (and backup stockings in case you rip yours) and jewelry and shoes and ties and makeup.

At the end of this book, I have charted the most common expenses you will have and left space for you to fill in a dollar amount of what you can realistically afford.

Additionally, in each of the following chapters, I will identify the hidden expenses related to that topic and offer ways you can save on those expenses.

Whenever you think about saving money, however, there is one axiom that holds true every time: in every way you find to save *money,* you will spend more in *time.* If you have more time than money, plus the inclination to do things yourself, the money savers may work perfectly for you. If you don't have the time or the inclination, you may be better off plunking down the bucks and getting it done to your satisfaction.

Determining Your Budget

Actually, "budget" is a good word, because it *is* going to "budge"—in some cases, by as much as 50 percent. More realistically, it will probably swell by about 15 to 20 percent more than you thought. Think of the budget as having an elastic band around it. Sometimes it feels as if it's being stretched to the bursting point, but most of us manage to keep it from breaking wide open.

Be realistic in determining your budget. There is no one ideal budget that works for everyone. Your budget will depend to a large extent on your environment. In some areas, it's very hard to spend less than $20,000 on a Bar/Bat Mitzvah; in others, you couldn't reach that amount if you tried. (Although I'm sure if *I* tried...)

You have to find the level at which you are comfortable, and then find out how much that is going to cost you in your neighborhood. Yes, you do have to put a price on your happiness. If what will satisfy you, your spouse, and child is a lovely luncheon for fifty people, check out restaurants or caterers and find out how much it will cost. If that doesn't do it, you need to go to the next level. Perhaps you really need to have a hundred and fifty people, *and* you need to have music and photographs. Explore the options and find out what those items will cost. Integrate the information into your value system and what you end up saying is, "I'm going to have to spend such-and-such amount of dollars to be who I am."

It's a good idea to affix a number, not just on your overall budget but within each category. Using the chart at the end of this book, you may be able to put a top dollar amount on each item—bearing in mind that (a) if you say you're going to spend no more than $150 on a dress for your daughter, you mustn't even go into a store where the only things you'll find for that amount are on the sale rack; (b) you probably will spend more than you figured; and (c) you can't have it all. Try to keep it within bounds. Even when it comes to money and your son or daughter's Bar/Bat Mitzvah, you *can* control your destiny.

Chapter Six

Timing: When to Hold Your Bar/Bat Mitzvah

One day, you may go to the mailbox and find a letter from your temple assigning you a Bar/Bat Mitzvah date. It could easily be three or even four *years* before your child turns thirteen. If you weren't expecting it, your reaction may range from mild amusement to out-and-out panic. "Why are they sending me this? My kid is in fourth grade! I'm not ready to know this yet!"

Guess what? In many communities, it's time to *get* ready. Temples that give out Bar/Bat Mitzvah dates years in advance are usually bending to local pressure: there are a lot of Jewish families in the community, there will be a good many Bar/Bat Mitzvahs, and frankly, by notifying you early, they're giving you a head start. You will have your choice of places to hold your reception, and there's less chance that you'll have to change because little Lisa's best friend Julie already has that date because *her* temple sent out the notice even earlier than yours.

Yes, in some areas it *is* a competition, and it's almost as if the catering halls were dictating the policy. Even if this doesn't apply to where you live, getting the date is still a signal. Don't stick the letter under a pile and forget about it; get the Bar/Bat Mitzvah ball rolling.

You're going to have to make several decisions about your child's ceremony almost as soon as you get—or choose—your date. The time and format of the reception is the first of those decisions and, arguably, the biggest. Once that's in place, you can relax. (Only kidding. You're Jewish. You're a mother. You can *never* relax.)

In some areas you *are* free to choose the date, time, and day of the week, but in many temples there isn't much choice. Whatever the policy, it's usually uniform: Bar/Bat Mitzvahs can take place only on Saturdays, for instance, or only on Friday nights or Sundays. It's rare to be able to change the day of the service. But you may be able to choose whether the service will be in the morning or the evening and, of course, when to have the reception. Many people choose to hold the reception immediately after the service; others, on a different day altogether. Here are some of the most popular choices, and some things to consider in making your decision.

Saturday Morning Services, Afternoon Reception

Many temples hold Bar/Bat Mitzvah ceremonies during the regular Saturday morning Shabbat service. The advantages of this arrangement are that everyone's fresh and there's less time to worry about things going wrong (okay, so you'll *make* time) and it's easy to plan a luncheon reception right afterward. An afternoon reception is usually more low-key and can feel like more of "a children's party." People tend to go straight from the services to the reception (you rarely have guests just going to one or the other), which makes for a nice continuity. People tend to be upbeat and not unduly tired. Usually there are few who leave early. Also, if your affair ends at five in the afternoon, it's easy to have people over at night (see Chapter 20) that you didn't really get to talk to during the party—to extend the wonderful day and joyous atmosphere as long as possible.

The disadvantage of an afternoon affair, if you're having it anyplace besides your home, is that it often *must* end at a prescribed time so the place can be readied for evening affairs taking place later. So even if you're having the time of your life and you want it to go on longer, you may not have that option.

Money-Saver Tip: If you've chosen to have your reception at a catering hall, hotel, or restaurant, a Saturday afternoon party is *less expensive* than one in the evening. Also, in some temples, it eliminates the need for a kiddush at the temple, and certainly you won't need a second set of clothing.

Saturday Morning Service, Evening Reception

People who go this route often want a nighttime party but don't have the choice of afternoon or evening temple services. They must hold the Bar/Bat Mitzvah ceremony in the morning. In some communities, that is the norm, but before you make this choice, remember: it an be difficult for guests who are driving from an hour or two away. Those coming from a greater distance usually have a place to stay. They can retire to their hotel rooms after the morning services and before the party. Those who live in the neighborhood have no problem; they just go home.

But those who are coming from an hour or so away are not going to go home—just to turn around and come back. You can invite them to your house, but you may not want a house full of people—or anyone outside the immediate family—there on that day. After all, you'll be preoccupied and busy. You may have beauty parlor appointments and a thousand tiny details to attend to. You may not be ready to play host right then. What often happens in this arrangement is that guests choose to attend either the service or the reception, not both. Which may not be what you want.

Another disadvantage: There's a break in the emotional action. During the ceremony you're flying high, proud and joyful and overwhelmed with emotion. Going straight home afterward can be a big let down, even though you'll be gearing up for the evening soon afterward. To some degree, you lose the momentum.

Hidden Cost Alert: It's more expensive to do it this way for several reasons. You may need to provide a kiddush for the congregation immediately following the service. An evening affair means dinner, which is more costly than lunch. You will need two sets of clothing and all that goes with the clothes: shoes, bag, jewelry, and so forth. *Another hidden cost:* many Bar/Bat Mitzvah families decide to spend the hours between the service and the party entertaining their out-of-town guests. There's a cost factor in there.

Clearly, the morning-and-evening way is more complicated, yet many people have no problem with it. If you're considering it, talk to those who've gone the route before.

Saturday Twilight Service, Evening Reception

If you want a nighttime party, it's nice to have a twilight or Havdalah service (the ritual that ends the Sabbath). That way, the flow from service to reception is uninterrupted. Twilight services can start as early as four P.M., at six, or even later, again depending on the policy at your synagogue. If it's an Orthodox one, services will start later during the spring, summer, and early fall months, which will force your reception to begin (and end) much later.

A nighttime reception is, no question, a bigger party. Some people need this event in order to fully celebrate: to be who they are and express their pride and joy in their Bar/Bat Mitzvah person. Nighttime receptions are more formal, regardless of the glitz factor. Many are black-tie events and seem to be geared toward the adults. Others are more low-key and just as much for the kids as the grown-ups.

Several factors integral to an evening reception could be viewed as disadvantages. People tend to get tired earlier, and there will be a higher percentage who leave early. If you're expecting a lot of elderly guests, the timing may be hard on them. Similarly, if you've invited a lot of children younger than your Bar/Bat Mitzvah child, it's going to be a strain on them—and on their parents. Of course, if you don't want a lot of little kids, this is a reasonable excuse not to invite them.

But even in terms of the thirteen-year-old contingent, while most won't have trouble staying up past midnight, you do have the problem of how they're getting home. Most hosts don't deal with it. Many a weary parent (usually the father) has climbed into the car at two A.M. to fetch his child from a nighttime Bar/Bat Mitzvah. Other hosts, however, do feel it's their responsibility to provide transportation home for the kids if the party runs very late. That's an *extra expense.* So is finding yourself springing for hotel rooms, not only for out-of-town guests, but for those with several hours on the road ahead of them.

Many of these issues depend on how responsible you feel for your guests. Some people feel very responsible; others, that the guests can make their own arrangements. Neither attitude is right or wrong. The point is knowing what yours is and factoring in the costs before you make your big decisions.

Other perceived disadvantages of a nighttime affair include the fact that at night, people tend to drink more, which may change the demeanor of the affair. It will certainly cost you more, for the same reasons as with the morning service/evening reception. One other thing you might want to think about: because it's a bigger, splashier party, people tend to dress up more. They arrive in temple dressed for a party, which some clergy find downright disrespectful. Tuxedos and bare-shouldered evening gowns, even for guests who are not participating, aren't exactly appropriate attire for a worship service. This may or may not bother you, but it is something else to think about.

Although most temples, regardless of affiliation, hold Bar and Bat Mitzvahs on Saturdays, some have other days. Here are some possibilities you may encounter.

Friday Night Service

In many congregations, you will find Bar and Bat Mitzvahs scheduled on Friday nights. If that is your temple's policy, your choice is terms of the reception is either to have a small celebration *before* or after the service, or on *another day* entirely. I have seen it done all ways. The main negative about having a party before the service is that it's hard for the Bar/Bat Mitzvah family to really relax and enjoy it, knowing the ceremony is still ahead. Having the reception afterward, you run into the same situation as with any evening event—except that many adults have worked during the day, many kids have had a full day of school, and they all tend to poop out earlier. Perhaps having an elaborate Oneg Shabbat afterward, and the reception on a later day, is the most popular choice in this situation.

Sunday Service

You won't find a boy being called to the Torah on a Sunday; there is no Torah service that day. You may, however, find yourself with a Sunday afternoon date for your daughter in a Bat Mitzvah service which parallels the boys' but isn't the same. The vast majority of people in this situation go right ahead and have the reception immediately following services that day. The major advantage is that (assuming you're hiring a caterer) it's traditionally cheaper on Sunday than anytime Saturday. The disadvantage is that people have work and school the next day, so they leave earlier.

Mondays/Thursdays

In some Orthodox congregations, parents have the choice of holding Bar Mitzvahs on these weekdays, along with the traditional Torah service. If you belong to this type of congregation, one advantage is clear: no one has to travel on the

Sabbath to share your simcha. The disadvantage is also clear if a party is part of the plan: a weekday/workday is not always conducive to a successful party. However, you can choose the Monday of a long secular holiday (Presidents' Week; spring break) or the Thursday (Thanksgiving) of a long weekend and have the same festive feel. Or, if that doesn't work, receptions for Monday/Thursday Bar Mitzvahs are simply held on another day.

Holidays

Technically, a Bar/Bat Mitzvah can take place any day there is a Torah service. That includes religious holidays. Although few people would seriously consider having a Bar/Bat Mitzvah on the High Holy days, there are other holidays that you might want to consider, assuming your temple is agreeable, such as Hanukkah, Pesach, or Sukkot. Depending on your community, often the children are out of school anyway. Choosing such a day might lend a festive atmosphere to your Bar/Bat Mitzvah and help make it extra special, significant, and memorable.

Chapter Seven

The Party Place and the Food

The only limitations on where to have your Bar/Bat Mitzvah reception are your imagination, your pocketbook, and your sense of appropriateness. Parties can be and have been held anywhere from the tiniest synagogue to a major league football stadium; from your own backyard to Club Med; on the high seas or high atop Massada in Israel (see Chapter 17). It all really depends on what kind of celebration you want.

Wide and varied though the choices may be, most of us, no matter what part of the world we live in, tend to choose from a few familiar formats. Here's what they are, the pros and cons of each, what you should be looking for, and the questions you should be asking about them.

A Kiddush at the Temple

Not only the least expensive way to go, for many people this is the only appropriate way. By catering (including making the food yourself) a lovely kiddush immediately following the service, you are absolutely fulfilling the traditional *seudah mitzvah*, the celebratory meal, after your child has been called to the Torah. You are extending the warmth and joyfulness of the occasion, and sharing it with those close to you and with the community.

Many families in which the parents are divorced choose this

as an alternative to a big party. It avoids many conflicts, financial and otherwise—whom to invite from his side/her side, who sits where, and so forth—that would be unavoidable with a big reception. However, many who choose this format often also have a children's-only get together later in the day, or on another day. More ideas along those lines can be found in Chapter 16.

This may seem the perfect solution if you're sincerely offended by the idea of big, lavish Bar/Bat Mitzvah parties. But consider this: a kiddush will end substantially sooner than a party, and very possibly before you're ready to let go of those wonderful emotions that are sure to wash over you when you see your child before the Torah. Simply put, a simple kiddush just may not do it for you.

An At-Home Reception

People tend to react very strongly to this choice: they see it either as the most intimate, traditional and best possible way to celebrate this event, *or,* as one person put it, "My idea of hell." Clearly, depending on your mind-set (some would say you're out of your mind if you're set on this), there are some heavy-duty pros and cons associated with this choice.

The Advantages: You have complete control over how much you will spend. Plus, everything is done your way. You decide on the food and either make it all yourself, have some help making it, or have it partially or completely catered. You settle on the timing: a few prescribed hours, or open house all day or all night long. You provide the decorations: it's your house and you don't have to have *any;* or you can transform it with flowers and/or balloons into anything you want. If you have the space, you can have music and dancing; you can certainly have a photographer/video person—in fact, all the trappings. You set the tone.

It is, no question, a more intimate affair. It's self-contained, there are no other parties going on, and you may have enough space for all age groups to feel comfortable.

It *can* be a very inexpensive alternative. If you're an intrepid do-it-yourselfer, you can have a ball spending months getting ready. You can pick and shop for and cook the food yourself (and freeze it); you can ask friends to help (this, in fact, is the tradition in many areas); you can fashion tablecloths and decorations, use fruit baskets for centerpieces, order flowers in bulk and wholesale. You can purchase just the amount (and kind of) liquor you need—which in itself can mean a considerable savings. For help in serving, you can hire local college students instead of professionals. Many a satisfying and wonderful at-home Bar/Bat Mitzvah has been celebrated in just this way.

The Disadvantages: It's a lot of work and can be extremely expensive. Only if you do everything yourself is it cheaper. The minute you start hiring and renting, you're in for a big financial surprise. In fact, having the celebration at home can be the *most expensive* way to do it. A backyard smorgasbord under the stars is a beautiful way to celebrate this milestone, but renting tents (you *must* consider the weather!), plus chairs, tables, linens, silverware, china, and glassware, doesn't come cheaply. Having to pay attention to all those details necessarily takes time that may be very hard to find, especially if you work outside the home and/or are devoting most of your time and energy to the Bar/Bat Mitzvah service itself.

If you're not cooking and serving yourself, you need a caterer and servers, and that of course involves time, effort, and money. Aside from the basic cost, you will also have to tip all this help. That can add up.

There may be space constraints at home. You may not have room for all the people you want to share the day with you. Even if you have a backyard, the weather may not be conducive to being outside. You may want music and dancing, but not have ample floor space, or seating.

You will be living with all this on a daily basis for months before, and cleaning up for who knows how long afterward. You will have the mess, and the headaches. You will have to handle all the details. There's no way it won't be disruptive to regular family life. Will it be worth it? That's up to you to decide.

A Reception at the Temple

For those who have mixed emotions about the appropriateness of a Bar/Bat Mitzvah party, or who want to keep their celebrations within at least a religious environment, a temple reception could be a perfect choice. And there are many advantages, not the least of which is that you don't have to travel anywhere after the service. Everyone is exactly where they need to be. They park one time, check their coats one time, and don't have to worry about digging up a second set of driving directions (not to mention that you don't have to print one up). You also don't have to transport your child's friends anywhere. Their parents drop them and pick them up at the same place. Especially after a Saturday morning service, a reception at the temple is simple and can be as elegant or as low-key as you want. An extra added plus: renting a room in a temple is usually very inexpensive. And since most temples have only one large reception room, yours will be the only affair going on at the time.

The temple also works if you're planning to go back into the sanctuary, for the *d'var Torah* and speeches by the guests, in between the smorgasbord and the main meal.

One very strong note of caution, however: only consider this if your temple has the facilities to host a reception *and* someone on staff with the experience to help you plan it. Some temples are well equipped to handle this event; they do it all the time and may even have their own caterer or are able to recommend someone. Others do not and are ill equipped for a reception. And all the wonderful reasons to choose the temple can easily be overshadowed by the headaches and tsuris (grief) you may have to deal with. I speak from experience.

For all the reasons detailed above, I wanted our son's Bar Mitzvah to take place at our temple. It seemed appropriate to me. I felt the atmosphere was low-key; it was convenient, pretty, and had a decent-sized space for dancing and enough room—if we kept the folding doors open and rented trellises—for our crowd of 140 people. Only later did I find out that I was pretty much on my own dealing with all the details, about four zillion of them. I was glad I had chosen a caterer who had worked at the temple before, because there were all sorts of rules and regulations I hadn't known about. But bringing an outside caterer into a temple not equipped for receptions meant, for example, that I had to rent chairs—the metal folding chairs available at the temple were uncomfortable and, frankly, ugly. And tables—there weren't enough of the right size.

What is more, there was tax on each chair, and each chair had to be insured. (Heaven forbid someone should fall off one of my rented chairs and sued.) I also had to rent separate tables to serve as bar stations, others specifically for the cocktail hour, and yet another on which to place the seating cards. The trellises were expensive, and decorating the room cost a fortune.

Naturally, there were rules about what you could hang (nothing, in fact) from the ceiling or walls, when the caterer could come to set up, when the florist could arrive, and when and where the photographer could set up shop. So much for my simple, low-key, stress-free affair! I'm not quarreling with the rules and regulations; it's a house of worship, after all, not a catering hall. And that's exactly what you must keep in mind when considering this alternative.

Other possible problems: if the synagogue is geared for this kind of occasion, you may have to use their caterer, whether or not you like it. Or you may have to use a kosher caterer—and that choice is more expensive. Or you might want to use a kosher caterer, but because the temple is Reform and your affair is to take place on a Saturday, the caterer may refuse. Finally, expect to run into time limitations and other hidden expenses. Talk with people who've done it before.

A Reception at a Hotel

Assuming you live in an urban or suburban area, a nice hotel experienced in receptions shouldn't be too hard to find. The trick, if you live in a non-Jewish area, may be finding one experienced in Bar/Bat Mitzvah receptions. One of the nicest I ever went to was in a Hilton about an hour outside of Chicago. Still, they had to fly the challah, the Sabbath bread, in from Chicago. At least they knew what it was; some places do not.

Aside from the relative ease in finding one, hotels have many other advantages. They have the facilities in place, there's less decorating to be done, certainly no rentals to deal with, and they can often alter the size of their ballrooms to fit your needs. Hotel catering directors are usually knowledgeable and experienced, which means fewer headaches for you. Best of all, perhaps, in many cases you can build your own menu. Many hotels do have set Bar/Bat Mitzvah menus and packages, but they may be willing to scrap them and provide only what you want, which could be cheaper in the long run.

Package deals can also serve as a negotiating point—before you sign the contract, that is. If the hotel throws in a Viennese dessert table as part of their deal and you really don't want one but do want more items for the cocktail hour, chances are you can substitute one for the other.

A hotel is your best choice if you have a lot of out-of-town guests. Not only will most hotels give you a substantial discount on the price of their rooms, they may also provide a hospitality suite at no charge (a nice place for your weary travelers to mingle) and perhaps a room for you to unwind or change clothes in.

My all-time favorite reason for choosing a hotel from a major chain is *points*. Many hotel chains offer promotions similar to those frequent-flyer points that airlines give out. Think how many points you can accumulate in one fell swoop with a

Bar/Bat Mitzvah reception: you could end up with enough for a free week's vacation stay. Seriously, ask about it. The hotels want your business.

The disadvantages start with the fact that hotels are expensive. They usually charge per person, a fee that includes liquor, based on what they think your guests will drink. The hotel doesn't lose money on the liquor; nine times out of ten, you're paying for much more than you actually consume. You may try to ask for a running tab on the bar and, that way, pay for only what your guests drink, but that assumes you trust the hotel's barkeeper and don't take into account that many of your guests (especially during the cocktail hour) will routinely take a few sips from a drink and put it down, move to another part of the room, then order another one. Most people who go the hotel route just pay the all-inclusive fee, knowing they're probably getting ripped off.

Money-Saving Tip: When booking a reception at a hotel make sure you pay less for every guest under twenty-one: they don't drink and you should not be charged the same rate as for adults.

Hidden Cost Alert: Before you sign the contract, check out the small print. Aside from your basic per-person cost, there is the tax. In each state, the tax rate and system are different, so find out first what it should be (for example, only on liquor but not on food or services) and make sure you're being charged fairly. If you're talking about a relatively big party, the tax can add up. There is also the matter of gratuities. Are they included? Who must be tipped? What if the service proves unacceptable? Iron all this out before you sign.

Other disadvantages associated with a hotel reception: catering is not their only business and may not be their strongest suit. There's less privacy. Your party is generally not the only one going on at any given time; you may even be able to hear the music from someone else's affair filtering through your set of folding doors. Not to mention someone else's Aunt Shirley popping up in one of your table pictures! (Does it really matter? Don't all families look the same anyway? Don't we all have Aunt Shirleys?)

A Reception at a Catering Hall

Choosing this alternative is similar on many counts to using a hotel ballroom. Many of the same advantages apply: everything is done for you; the staff is experienced and may be able to educate you and offer insight; there's less decorating, no rentals, everything's in place, they do this all the time. In fact, that's a major advantage, even over a hotel: catering is *all* they do. It's their only business, and to stay in business they had better be good at it. Nearly all their business is from referrals. Don't think they don't know that half the guests at your Bar/Bat Mitzvah have their own coming up: catering halls very much want to impress.

You can negotiate with them. Often they will throw in extras just to clinch the deal: caviar at the cocktail hour, valet parking, flowers already on the tables. (If you chose not to use their flowers, they may give you a per-table credit.) In many cases they *may* be more economical than hotels; comparison shopping is the best way to find out.

Because caterers have seen many Bar/Bat Mitzvahs, they may be able to suggest reputable and reasonable florists, musicians, and photographers and steer you away from those who don't do good work. Yes, it's possible that these caterers get kickbacks, but if the price is right and the work looks good, it may not matter.

The disadvantages of choosing a catering hall are again similar to those at a hotel: it can be expensive (although the expense tends to vary more at catering halls); it can feel impersonal; there may be other affairs going on at the same time. The same hidden expenses apply, vis-à-vis liquor, taxes, and tips.

Receptions at Restaurants and Other Imaginative Places

Though the alternatives detailed above are the most common ones, there are many other routes to take that are just as nice, less (though sometimes more!) expensive, and with the added cachet of being unique. A *scenic restaurant* can provide a beautiful setting for your simcha. It works especially well if you have a small group and want an intimate feeling (usually, you're the only party) but don't want to have the affair at home. Restaurants are often less expensive than catering halls or hotels, and many are known for the quality of their food. If that's of utmost importance to you, and you're not looking to throw a big blowout with music and smoke machines, this may be your answer. When surveying the possibilities in your area, however, you'll want to ask how experienced the restaurant is with Bar/Bat Mitzvah parties: you may want to think twice if they don't know from challah, chopped liver, or the candle-lighting ceremony.

A restaurant may also work best if you're putting the affair together on short notice. Most restaurants don't book affairs very far in advance and are more likely than catering halls or hotels to be available. Conversely, if you *are* booking two and three years ahead of time, it may be difficult to find a restaurant willing to make that commitment.

Boats, ferry boats, and even *yachts* have been used for Bar/Bat Mitzvah parties, which, weather cooperating, have been wonderfully successful—and not always that expensive. Of course, you do have to be realistic about the season and optimistic about the weather. Being raised up on a chair during the hora dance with the possibility of going overboard is not my idea of fun.

Other ideas: you could rent out a *social hall* (women's clubs, YM-YWHA's, etc.) in your area, usually for a nominal fee, and bring in your own caterer, decorations, and music. If you belong to a *country club,* you might want to check out those facilities (even if you don't belong, many are willing to rent out their ballrooms and facilities).

I have heard of Bar/Bat Mitzvah parties being held in old *brownstones,* in *mansions, town houses, private gardens,* in *lofts,* in a *castle* (oy vay—without electricity!), on a dude ranch—with hayrides and barbeque—at *tennis clubs, health clubs, nightclubs, discos,* even at *West Point Military Academy,* the *Children's Museum of Boston,* and *art galleries* in Washington, D.C. Many of these ideas work best if you're just planning a children's party—again, check out Chapter 16 for more ideas.

Then, many people spread their Bar/Bat Mitzvah celebrations over entire weekends, taking their guests to a resort hotel, a summer camp, a retreat, or even Club Med. It sounds terrifically extravagant, but if you limit the guest list to just close family members and a few friends, you could end up spending the same amount on a weekend shindig as you would on two hundred people at the Hilton for five hours.

If you're looking even further afield for ideas, there is a book called *Places* that describes interesting and unique party spaces in ten major metropolitan areas. It's available in most large bookstores, or you can write to: Tenth House Enterprises, Box 810, Gracie Station, New York, NY 10028, to find out if your city is represented.

What You Should Be Looking For and Asking About

The Place

- The *size of the room* you are booking: is it big enough for your crowd, or too big? You don't want tables so close together that people can't maneuver around them (especially at a buffet where people are carrying plates of food). You also don't want your fifty people to feel swallowed up in a room that accommodates a hundred and fifty.
- The size of the *dance floor.* Nothing puts a damper on what

could be a lively party so much as not having room to do the Electric Slide (or whatever the hot dance is at the moment). If you've got a dancing crowd, make sure they have enough room to cut loose.

- If you're planning a *cocktail hour,* where will that be held? Is the space adequate and attractive? In many hotels especially, I've seen lovely ballrooms, but the cocktail hour is often held in a hallway.
- *Cleanliness,* not only of the room you're using, but the lobby *and* the bathrooms. In addition, where *are* the mens' and ladies' rooms? Are they easily accessible? Many of your guests will be visiting that facility at least once during a five-hour party.
- Adequate *coat-check* facility and staff. Sounds picayune, but not when people are wearing expensive wraps.
- *Wheelchair accessibility* for those guests who may need it.
- *Ratio of servers* to tables. In a sit-down dinner situation, three servers per two tables works exceptionally well.
- If you're going straight from the temple, *how long is the drive* to the party place? Will it be hard for guests unfamiliar with the area to find? Most people try to keep travel time under thirty minutes and choose a place that is fairly accessible.
- Is the place used to *hosting Bar/Bat Mitzvahs,* or do they do mostly weddings?
- How many *other parties* will be going on at the same time as your celebration, and how close will the parties be? What's the noise factor? Will you be hearing the hora from another party while you're tearily slow-dancing to "Wind Beneath My Wings?"
- What's the *atmosphere of the place like?* How is the lighting? If you don't want people to know if it's day or night (and really lose themselves in the party), does the place feature nightclub lighting? Or, if you like light, bright, open spaces, does the place offer that? Weather permitting, can you have any part of your reception (the cocktail hour, for instance) outdoors?
- What's the *parking* situation? If there isn't valet parking,

will it be easy for your guests to find a spot and walk—some in high heels—to the front door? If there *is* valet parking, is it free?

- Last but definitely not least, *how long have they been in business,* what is their reputation, and are there any rumors about the proprietor going out of business? What happens if you've booked two years in advance and suddenly the place goes belly-up? For one thing, you lose your deposit. For another, you've got to find another place, and quickly.

The Food

- *Taste it first!* Any caterer—off-premise, or in a hotel, catering hall, or restaurant—that refuses to let you taste the food before deciding is not worth considering. You have to wonder what they're hiding. Many caterers, eager for your business, will prepare an entire meal for you. (Of course, then you might feel guilty about not choosing them—but then, there's always something to feel guilty about. It comes with the territory.)

- What are your *choices* and what is the price range? Many caterers will quote you a price based on the cheapest entree and then go on to extol the virtues of their "award-winning" chateaubriand, for ten dollars more a person. (Funny, we never think to ask who gave them the award, and for what.) Is there enough variety of different types, something for everyone, the eight- to the eighty-year-olds?

- Will there be a *cocktail hour,* and what foods will be offered? Will it be in a smorgasbord setup entirely, or will there be pass-around hors d'oeuvres, served butler style? How much staff will there be at the cocktail hour?

- *Rule of thumb vis-à-vis food:* People will *eat more and drink less* at a luncheon affair, especially if you're coming straight from a morning service. Many have rushed out of the house without breakfast, so by the time they get to the cocktail hour they're starving. Offering more variety at that point will be appreciated. People will *drink more and eat less* at night: they've been eating all day, now they want to party.

- What is the difference, in terms of cost, variety of food, and comfort of guests between a *buffet* and *sit-down* dinner? There are pros and cons to both. Find out what they say at the place you're considering. Some are highly skilled at buffets and guests don't have to stand on long lines; others don't encourage it because they don't do it very well. Don't automatically assume that buffets are cheaper. Often they're more expensive, because there's more food and it takes more staff to run them well.

- Buffets lend a more low-key feel to your event, and often there is greater variety of food. In addition, a buffet forces people to get up and mingle, where with a sit-down dinner, many people just sit down, and never move. You have to decide if you care or not. And you have to decide what *you* like. Most older people prefer to be served, but if they're there to share the joy of the day with you, they really shouldn't mind a little inconvenience—if it is that. For a buffet, however, you may want to rethink the cocktail hour: will it be too much of the same?

- At a sit-down, how will the food be *served:* family style, French style, or something in between? What's the policy about seconds? In some instances, especially with an off-premise caterer, they only bring enough for the number of people you've told them; there *are* no seconds. In other situations, the food is unlimited.

- How is the food presented? Can you drop in on someone else's affair *before it starts* to see for yourself?

- What is the policy regarding kosher vs. kosher style vs. nonkosher? If you need to be kosher, expect to pay more, especially if you're bringing a kosher caterer into another facility. Profits then get split several ways and the cost to you goes up.

- Can you arrange to have your leftovers donated, say, to local shelters for the needy and homeless? Some caterers will allow you to do that. Others say they can't. If this is something you feel strongly about, check out the policy first.

The Caterer

Whether you're considering an off-premise caterer, or one in a hotel, restaurant, or catering hall, there are three things to consider above all else:

First, caterers live or die on their *reputations*. They had better be good. Always ask around first, before you even make an appointment to see the person.

Second, how long have they been in business? How much *experience* do they have? You don't want to be their first Bar/Bat Mitzvah.

Finally come *flexibility and cooperation*. Whose affair is it, theirs or yours? A great many caterers who fulfill the first two requirements are just plain bullies. You do it *their* way: they know what to serve, how to serve it, and when to stop the hora because the fruit salad must be eaten at that moment (seriously, this has happened). No matter how long their years of experience, *you* are the customer. The best caterer is a pro who is willing to be both cooperative and flexible.

Some caterers are very helpful. They will guide you in terms of an overall timetable for your affair, counsel about seating plans (and not be inflexible about the number of people you may have at a table), help you figure out the timing of the event, and set up a reasonable payment plan. That's the kind you want. Others leave you on your own, then tell you they can't do it that way. That's the kind you don't want.

Other things to think or ask about:

In a hotel situation, you may develop a rapport with a staff caterer, only to find out he or she is no longer there when your affair rolls around. That is less likely to happen at a catering hall or with an off-premises caterer.

Will the person with whom you've been working attend your affair, or will there suddenly be an unfamiliar face to handle everything?

If you're thinking of an off-premises caterer, has he or she worked at the facility before? There's a lot less grief for you if the caterer already knows the rules, regulations, and requirements (often they must be insured for a specific dollar amount) of the place you want.

How the children will be accommodated may also help determine the place you chose for your reception. You might want to ask:

- Is there a separate space for the kids to be during the cocktail hour? Often, they appreciate being able to mingle among themselves at that point in the party.
- Is there a separate kids' menu? Youngsters generally prefer chicken, french fries, mini-pizzas, spaghetti, or pigs-in-blankets to salmon croquettes and veal Oscar. (Actually, so do most adults, given the choice.)
- Must the children sit on a dais, or do they have the option of sitting at tables as adults do? Some Bar/Bat Mitzvah candidates have their own preference about that.
- Is there adequate supervision? Especially at parties with a lot of youngsters, some will inevitably get wild. Some places are better equipped to handle this (*you* shouldn't have to play cop on this day), and provide matrons in the ladies' room and someone to supervise the making of the "memory" glass. (Popular at Bat Mitzvahs, friends of the girl collect small souvenirs from the party, stash them in a glass, and melt candles over it to seal it—which has resulted in more than one fire, ergo the need for supervision.)

Money-Saving Tips

If you're going the catering hall or restaurant or hotel route:

If you have a choice of dates, picking a place during its slow season (January/February or July) may save you quite a few bucks.

Sundays are cheaper than Saturdays. Saturday lunch is cheaper than Saturday dinner.

Poultry is cheaper than prime rib.

You *can* say (but nicely!) "So and So Catering throws in three more hors d'oeuvres. Can you match it?"

If you've given a reception at the place before, will they offer you a second-time-around discount? Many places will.

Aside from charging less for children, many places also do not charge anything for children under six or seven (how much are they really going to eat?) and charge less for elderly guests seventy and over. Ask.

There exists something called Catered Affair Cancellation Insurance, just in case, due to illness or a tornado, you do have to cancel or postpone your affair. Ask your caterer about it. Or ask your insurance agent.

If you're going the off-premises (temple, social hall, etc.) or at-home route but with a caterer:

- Can you provide the liquor yourself? Not only will it be a lot cheaper, but there are liquor stores that will allow you to *bring back* unopened bottles for a refund. Could be a major savings.
- Does the caterer have breakage insurance? What if, at your house, they smash a valuable vase?

A major overall rule of thumb, no matter what kind of place you choose, is to talk to people who've done it before. *Know* what you're getting into. The best surprise on that magic day is no surprise.

Finally, are you overwhelmed already, just reading this chapter? Consider a *party planner*. If you've got more money than time, and don't want to or can't do the legwork yourself, think about hiring a party planner to do it for you. They have lists reputable caterers, decorators, musicians, photographers, invitations, and so forth—at their fingertips.

Party planners always work within your budget. Some charge a percentage of the total budget; others, a flat fee. Naturally, using a party planner is going to be more expensive than doing all this yourself. But if you work, if you're single, if you really can't deal with it, but want a fabulous party, this may be the answer to your prayers.

Chapter Eight

The Guest List

Along with picking a place and a format for your Bar/Bat Mitzvah, you will have to start drawing up a guest list. In fact, you need to know how many people you're inviting before you can decide on much of anything else.

There are basically two ways to go about devising your guest list. You can settle on a budget and format first ($10,000 at a catering hall) and then see how many people you can afford to invite. Or (and more commonly), you can see who in your life you want to share this joyous occasion with and then hope you can afford to invite 'em all!

Make a List—Make Lots of Lists

Typically, we open up our address books, flip through the Rolodex, and start listing. Your list (and that of your spouse or co-planner) will naturally include the Bar/Bat Mitzvah child's grandparents, great-grandparents (if you're lucky), uncles, aunts, and cousins. You'll have your friends and relatives, your not-so-close friends (but you want them there anyway), the pay-backs (people who invited you, so you have to reciprocate), and people from work. Pretty simple, huh? Just wait.

Next, the Bar/Bat Mitzvah *child* makes a list. No matter how long *your* list is, this one will be longer. It will include best friends, school friends, Hebrew school friends, camp friends, friends of friends, kids who've invited them, kids they *think* might invite them, and the cute kid he/she has a crush on that sits next to them in Science. You're not finished yet.

Now we come to the lists—you'll get these without asking—from your own parents and in-laws. In many cases, they are perfectly reasonable and include people you really want to be there. And then there are the other cases, lists of people not only you never heard of (let alone the Bar/Bat Mitzvah child) but whose first names your in-laws aren't even sure of. Still, they *have* to be invited. You mean you didn't even *know* you had an Uncle Harry in Paducah? Your mother isn't sure which wife he's on, or what her name is. But no matter. There they are, on that list. See why this is beginning to be not so simple?

Okay, you've got your lists. Add them all up and if you're like most of us, you've got a grand total of about two thousand people, or the entire population of Naperville, Illinois. (What, you forgot about that long-lost relative *in* Naperville? Oops, two thousand and one.)

Slicing and Dicing: How to Cut the Lists Down

Now comes the fun part: Who ya' gonna cut? And the battle royals: if not between you and your spouse (of course, if it's an ex-spouse you're more likely to use this as a battleground), then certainly between you and your child, and often between you and your parents and in-laws.

Since most of us really can't afford to invite everyone on those lists, we need some cutoff strategy. Some people just make a blanket decision that all relatives up to second cousins will be invited and that's it. Or, nobody will be invited that you haven't spoken to in the last several years, regardless of how close you are biologically. Others slash an entire category: no one from the office. (That has an advantage in that you can explain it was only friends and relatives; fewer feelings may get hurt that way.) But being so cut-and-dried doesn't always leave you with a list of people you want there. That's why most of us have a harder time of it.

The criteria I used were simple: we would invite people who had a relationship with my child and people who were truly happy for us and wanted to share this day. That meant some relatives, but not others; some people from the office, but not everyone; and most of our friends, but few acquaintances. There weren't too many disagreements with my spouse. If he felt really strongly about someone, I didn't argue, and vice versa. But admittedly, sometimes it did become like a trading game: "I'll trade you Bruce and Sarah for Neil and Melanie," or, "If you give up Lou and Audrey, I'll give up Dan and Sandy."

A friend of mine invited third cousins but not all second cousins, the rationale being that the third cousins were kids the same age as the Bat Mitzvah girl and he wanted to perpetuate the generations by bringing those cousins closer.

While you might have a relatively easy time paring your list, wait until you try talking your Bar/Bat Mitzvah child into making some cuts. You might as well be asking them to relinquish the remote control. They'll present a hundred good reasons for keeping each one on the list—and then end the argument with the oft-repeated phrase, "It's *my* day." You can try reasoning, you can try bribery, or any of the other tactics that have worked before, but as long as their total doesn't threaten to become the whole party—and if you can afford it— you might consider letting them have everyone they want. Or you could pick a reasonable number and say, "No more than thirty friends. That's it. You decide."

I will say this, looking back on the Bar/Bat Mitzvahs of my son and daughter. At the time, they came up with some very unfamiliar names, youngsters I'd never heard of or seen before. But afterward, some of those youngsters ended up becoming their close friends: inviting them to their Bar/Bat Mitzvahs was my kids' way of making friends with them.

In terms of your own parents and in-laws, the deal you strike basically depends on (a) your relationship with them and (b) how much you can afford. You might feel that, well, this is their simcha too, and they're entitled to invite whomever they want;

that's a lovely thought, but it only works well if they haven't invited the entire retirement community and money isn't an issue. If you still want them to have their friends there, but can't afford it, you could ask them to pay for a certain number of their own guests. That's not unheard-of. Or you could just say, "Mom, Dad, we want you to have the best day ever. Here's how many people you can invite," and give them a number. Most parents will understand and not give you a hard time.

Sticky Situations

What if only some members of a family have a relationship with you and the Bar/Bat Mitzvah child? Can you break up families?

That depends on whom you're thinking of leaving out. If it's a younger child, you may put the parents in a bind: it truly may be hard for them to bring one and leave one home. If it's an older teenager or college student, they may feel uncomfortable coming anyway and you may be doing them all a favor by leaving them out. If the family is close enough, call and let them in on your thinking. Their reactions may help you make your decision.

What about divorced relatives; do you invite them both?

If you still have a relationship and/or warm feelings toward both people, you certainly can. They're adults; they'll deal with it.

What about singles who call and ask to bring a guest?

If you've addressed the invitation to them alone, one assumes you didn't count on them bringing a guest. How you respond depends on your relationship to the person and how many other singles call with the same request. If each brings a guest and that brings your total up way higher than you anticipated, you've got a problem and should just say no. But if it's only a few people and you know it will make them much more comfortable, it's nice to answer yes.

There's a little saying that captures my feelings on the whole issue of whom to ask to share this day. Wait until the last minute, and then, "When in doubt, invite." If you've wrestled with this for a while, and there are certain people whose names still keep coming up but you're still unsure of, you'll probably feel better in the long run inviting them. Usually, it's just a few people and not worth the hard feelings in the end if you leave them out.

And if, when all is said and done, you've still got many more people than you can possibly afford, rethink the format and settle for something less elaborate. The *people* are more important than the place, or the kind of party you have.

Yeah, But Half of Them Won't Come Anyway

Just drawing up the list isn't the whole story, however. Although, on average, fifteen percent of the people you invite will decline your invitation, it's not always the ones you thought ("Oh, we were planning to come in from Bora Bora anyway on just that day—how lucky!") and you really should be prepared just in case they *all* decide to show up. If you really can't afford to pay for more than a hundred people, don't invite a hundred and thirty.

Obviously, a lot depends on geography, the percentage of elderly people you're inviting, and the time of year. If most of your family are octogenarians living in Florida and your affair is up North in January, it's a pretty safe bet that they won't come. If your Bar/Bat Mitzvah is in the spring or fall, don't count the seniors out.

The Danger of "A" and "B" Lists

In theory, it sounds good. You divide everyone you want to invite into two lists. On the A list, put the definites and the ones you're sure won't come. Then, when you get regrets, quickly invite someone from the B list, which includes everyone else you wanted to invite in the first place, but couldn't. Never works. Either the people you're sure wouldn't come say they will, or by the time they RSVP it's too late to bring in your pinch hitters. You've got to have one list and go with that.

Last-Minute Cancellations

What you *can* be absolutely sure of, but can do nothing about, are last-minute cancellations. Depending on the weather and the distance, it's usually anywhere from one or two couples to—in our case—a whopping twelve people who didn't show up. Some called early that morning; others sent regrets with another guest; one elderly uncle missed his ride. My Chicago relatives missed the plane, a cousin's back went out, a friend came down with food poisoning, and so on. It so happened that all the kids came, but they're often the main culprits when it comes to no-shows. They goofed up the date (the invitation came, they sent it back without showing their parents, only to find out too late that mom and dad had other plans).

You know what? At that point, it doesn't really matter. Hopefully, the important people are there—the ones you really care about—and there's nothing you can do about it anyway. In the rare case a no-show will spoil your day (they may spoil your perfect seating arrangements, but that's another chapter).

Keeping Track of Your List: Categorize, Alphabetize, Computerize!

You've got to have some system for tracking your invitees. The first time, I really didn't, and what a lot of extra headaches! There are many ways to do this, depending on just how sophisticated you want to get.

Some people use index cards, others long yellow pads, others buy a loose-leaf notebook, and those with computer savvy create a database. Whatever your system is, it's best to break your list into categories: your friends, your relatives, spouse's relatives, friends of the child, business associates, guests of your parents, guests of your in-laws. Within each list, alphabetize: it will make things go much faster.

The best systems are the simplest. Using colored 3 × 5 index cards, one color for adults (one card per couple) and another color for children, print names and addresses, if they RSVP'd, what gift they gave, and whether a thank-you was sent or not. Arrange the cards alphabetically. As soon as you get a "No," put that card aside. When all the RSVP's come in, it's easy to add up how many adults and how many children there will be. The other plus to doing it this way: the cards are portable and if you need to take them to your parents' or in-laws' to discuss the guest list, it's easy. You can also use the same cards for addressing thank-you's *and* for seating. Just put them on the floor and play. (Actually, seating is never easy, but again, that's another chapter.)

Another system involves putting the PC to good use (and you thought you'd never use it). Using the spreadsheet (Lotus) program, you list your guests and create categories, same as you would on the index cards. The beauty is that the computer alphabetizes for you (although one of my friends got the names alphabetized, but forgot to tell the computer to move the addresses along with it) and keeps track automatically of your changing totals (both for adults and children *and* cost of each). This is how one friend described her computer system: "I used the database of . . . Appleworks and set up a file for each guest: name, address, number of guests, reply, brunch invitation, hotel, double or king-size beds, name list for placecards and favors, tables assigned, gifts, thank-you sent." Admittedly, this person loves using her computer and loves to organize. When the time came to make seating arrangements, she printed out the list, cut it up, and played, moving people to this table and that.

If all of this sounds much too complicated, you can use a simple yellow pad with ruler-drawn columns, as I did, and put in the pertinent information.

The Out-of-Towners

The lengths you go to make out-of-town guests feel comfortable depends on how many you're expecting, how close they are to you, and once again, that old devil, money. How much you're willing to spend, that is. At any rate, it's nice to give these guests some idea of their options in terms of accommodations *when you send the invitation.* It will help them decide whether to come or not.

If you're planning to put people up in your home, let them know. If you've made arrangements for them to stay with friends, advise them of that option. If you're planning to make hotel reservations, they should be aware of that too. Working with the hotel, you might enclose a little card with their invitation saying, "We have reserved a block of rooms at the Park Ridge Marriott Hotel. Please fill out this card and return it to the hotel if you're planning on attending." *If you can,* it's a nice touch to pay for their rooms. If you can't, don't worry about it; most people aren't expecting it. Either way, you should make the arrangements, because you know the area.

Money-Saving Tip: Some hotels will give you a break if you're reserving several rooms. Others—for a nominal fee, or even for free—will transport your guests from the airport, and/or from the hotel to the temple or reception. *Ask* when you make the reservations; they usually don't volunteer this kind of information.

The nicest out-of-town Bat Mitzvah I was ever invited to took place in a distant suburb of Chicago. *Along with the invitation* came a separate, typewritten note, not only advising us that hotel reservations had been made, but giving us instructions every step of the way. The note said something like: "Welcome to Deborah's Bat Mitzvah. Let us know what flight you are on and we will send transportation for you to the hotel. At nine A.M. the next morning, be in the lobby. You will be picked up and brought to the temple." We never had to make any arrangements ourselves, we never had to wonder how to get from one place to another, we never had to spend a dime (aside from our air fare). Knowing all that, it was easy to make our decision. Of course we went, and we had a wonderful, memorable weekend.

The cousin who arranged all this put a lot of work into it, and all those arrangements did cost her a bundle. But she also had a lot of out-of-town relatives and the same system worked for all.

Even if you don't go to such lengths to make your out-of-towners comfortable, a nice touch when they arrive is to have a basket or "info packet" in their hotel room with directions and instructions (to the temple from the hotel, and so forth) and a little note to welcome them. *That* shouldn't cost you much at all, and will be much appreciated.

Chapter Nine

The Invitations

One of the most joyous tasks before you is inviting the people you love to come and share the day. Any way you chose to do it, by informal, handwritten note all the way to a video production extravaganza (yes, it's been done, and wait until you hear about it), is perfectly acceptable, as long as you get the "who, what, where, and when" main points across.

Invitation Timetable

Unless your service and reception are very informal, and there aren't many others in your area, you should follow a basic timetable. Here is one suggestion, into which I've built plenty of time. Obviously, you can make certain adjustments based on the tradition in your neighborhood.

- *Eight months before your Bar/Bat Mitzvah:* start looking for invitations and decide whether to purchase the preprinted, out-of-the-books type or to create your own.
- *Six months before:* Order the invites, or start making them. Many take a long time; others you'll have in a jiffy. Sometimes orders arrive with mistakes and have to be sent back and reordered. Play it safe: order early.
- *Three months before:* You should have them in hand. It sounds awfully early, but consider: you may need this time if you're using a calligrapher, if you want to use special

postage stamps, *and* to get everything (including directions cards) together and start stuffing the envelopes.

- *Two months before:* Mail them. If you're in an area where the kids get invited to a lot of Bar/Bat Mitzvahs, or it's summertime and people are away, you might even want to mail them ten weeks ahead of time. If Bar/Bat Mitzvahs are scarce in your area, it's perfectly acceptable to mail them seven or even six weeks before the date.
- *Three weeks before:* You should have your responses back. If it's to be a formal reception, the caterer will need a head count (not the final one, but a ballpark figure) about two weeks to ten days ahead. You also have to allow time for late respondents, and most important, to give *yourself* time to set up seating, candle lighting, and even choosing people for honors and aliyot. None of which you can finalize until you know who's coming.

Where to Find Invitations

Most people do it by the book—several books, that is. Stationery stores, party stores, the temple gift shop or sisterhood, and very often private people working out of their homes carry books filled with invitations. Look for ads in Jewish publications; ask around.

Some books carry all kinds of invites—for weddings, sweet sixteen parties, surprise parties, and so on—but there are specialty books that carry only Bar/Bat Mitzvah ones. You will find some bearing religious symbols and quotes from the Scriptures, others that are completely secular—styles vary wildly. As do prices: you might want to check out a few books first, before bringing your child to look, and eliminate entire books (or stores, for that matter) that are just too pricey.

Even if you're going to design your own invitation, looking through books will give you ideas for illustrations and wording.

A handmade invitation has the advantage of allowing you to express a personal theme. One idea is to work with a rabbi and local artist to illustrate the theme that every generation is a link in the chain of tradition tied to the Torah. Your design could also feature the Bar/Bat Mitzvah's own artwork or poetry.

Of course, books needn't be your only resource. I have not only received but heard about invitations that were incredibly creative; some were also incredibly expensive, but others were not. Bar/Bat Mitzvah invitations have come engraved on marble slabs (imagine the postage!), Lucite blocks, or brass plaques; in a can (that one was cute: you opened the pop-top and out popped several cards bearing the pertinent information); in a toy jeep (it was sort of a jungle-safari theme); as a puzzle with movable parts; with a photograph of the child superimposed over the wording; as a giant collage; and in a three-dimensional scene with pop-up instructions.

There have been invitations on audio tape, and my all-time favorite, the video invitation to "Jonathan's Bar Mitzvah." Warm, imaginative, informative, and a family production, there's no way this one could have cost a great deal—except possibly to mail. Dad got hold of a camcorder and videotaped thirteen-year-old Jonathan inviting you to his Bar Mitzvah. Jonathan not only gave the date and time, but went through an entire review of his haftarah. Next came Jonathan's sister Lisa, all dressed up and cute as a button. It was her job to tell where and when the reception was being held.

The pièce de résistance of this video extravaganza, however, was the driving directions. Made by mounting the camcorder on the dashboard of the family car, the video took guests from the major highways through every bend in the road, every turn, street sign, and stoplight along the way, pointing out scenery and even cautioning you to watch out for trucks and not to speed—all the way to the temple. Using the same procedure, the video then took you from the temple to the reception. Of course, unless you travel with a VCR and monitor in the car, I don't quite know of what use it all was. But it was original, memorable, and probably cost-effective.

What to Say

Most invitations are worded pretty similarly, often starting with, "Please join us as we celebrate the Bar Mitzvah of our son," or "It is our pleasure to invite you to worship with us at the Bat Mitzvah of our daughter," or "Please share a special moment in our lives as our son, Michael, is called to the Torah." In the case of a divorced family, the invitation might start with, "My family and I invite you to worship with us when I am called to the Torah."

You must include:

1. The *name of the child.*
2. *The date* (and the year).
3. *The time* (it's advisable, and often temple policy anyway, to ask your guests to arrive a half hour before services actually begin; that allows time for latecomers not to disturb the service in progress and for the inevitable happy schmoozing).
4. *The place* (you might skip the full address of the temple—especially if you want to save space—because by necessity, it will be on the directions card).

The invitation will be signed by you and your spouse, except possibly when the parents are divorced, in which case it can be signed by the child him/herself, or the names of the parents may be on separate lines, so instead of "Marvin & Randi Reisfeld," it might look like: Marvin Reisfeld
                                    Randi Reisfeld

If applicable, you will want *reception information,* either on the invitation or on a separate insert. If the reception is to follow the services immediately, it is often preferable to print that on the invitation itself. If your reception plans are a little more complicated—say, you're having a kiddush or brunch after the service, and a reception later on—it's advisable to use a separate insert.

Most invitations also include a way for your guests to *RSVP*, and driving *directions*.

The best way to figure out exactly how to word your invitation is by reading others for inspiration. Looking through books can be helpful; among the samples there will be variations on wording. Even easier is looking at invitations your child has received. I simply went into my daughter's room, where she had at least a dozen invitations on her wall, and cribbed from those. (Naturally, she vetoed my choice and we ended up using the shmaltzy wording she wanted.)

Studying other invitations also will give you a sense of where to break the lines, which words to capitalize, where the placement of the words should go—all decisions you'll have to make when ordering. It really is a good idea to come prepared with everything written out exactly as you want it before you place your order. That way, there's less chance of mistakes. And they do occur. One very intelligent friend of mine ordered beautiful invitations that she and her daughter had finally chosen after weeks of looking. They chose the wording, approved everything, and the order was put through. Only when the invitations came back did anyone realize they'd neglected to include the time. Quickly, extra inserts (at extra cost) had to be made up and mailed out with the invitations.

Proofread carefully before you put the order through!

Directions Cards

Included in your packet will be directions cards. Many temples have them preprinted, which you are welcome to use. If you're holding a reception somewhere other than the temple, you'll need directions there as well; many hotels, restaurants, and catering halls also provide them.

What no one will provide, however—and what many people forget to include on their directions cards—is how you get *from the temple to the reception.*

If your reception immediately follows the service, that is key information for your guests, and you will have to get in the car, follow the route, and make up those directions yourself. Be specific; write down landmarks as well as mileage. Travel it more than once and have someone else familiar with the neighborhood check what you've written. Include the exact addresses and phone numbers of the temple *and* the party place, even if it's your own home. It's also a nice touch to add instructions leading your guests back to the major roads and highways to help them get home. For example, "Leaving Carrie's party, turn left out of the parking lot and go two miles to the Garden State Parkway...."

You might xerox a map with the routes highlighted and put in approximate travel times, such as "It should take ten minutes to get from Pascack Road to Route 17...."

Once you've got all your data together, it needs to be typed and xeroxed, offset or keyboarded on the word processor, and printed.

Another bit of information that's useful to have on your directions cards might advise parents, "A ride for Matthew's friends will be provided from the temple to the Hilton." And, "Please arrange to have your child picked up at the Hilton at approximately six P.M." This can save a ton of last-minute phone calls.

Response Cards

If your Bar/Bat Mitzvah is to be very informal, it is perfectly acceptable to include your telephone number on the invitation after the date by which you need an RSVP. If you're inviting a lot of people and it will be more formal, it's customary to include a separate response card in your invitation packet.

Generally, the wording is very simple: "Kindly respond by _____." (As noted before, two and even three weeks before the

Bar/Bat Mitzvah is a good date to give.) Most often, the response card is sent with a preprinted envelope bearing your name and address (or the child's if that's who signed the invitation). It's customary for you to prestamp it as well.

When you send response cards, you not only expect people to let you know if they are attending, but also—this sounds ridiculous, but hear me out—*who* they are. In other words, you naturally assume people will sign their names. Believe it or not, many don't! Whether they're just absentminded, have never done this before, think you have ESP, or think they're being cute, you can count on getting back at least a few cards that say, "We'll be there," with nothing else on the card, or, "Sorry, we can't make it," unsigned.

That's why it's a good idea, albeit time-consuming, to number or otherwise code your response cards. Using a pen (not a pencil, because those "cute" people—okay, like me—will erase it), number each card, either on the back, tucked away discreetly inside the envelope, or, if you want to get cagey, under the stamp or in invisible ink. Concurrently, on your guest list, add their response card number next to their names.

In some circles it's become a tradition to find creative ways of sending back response cards. They're returned unsigned but with a clue-filled poem; with balloons attached ("We'll be floating on air to Mindy's Bat Mitzvah"); with cookies; in the form of a crossword puzzle or acronym; on a homemade video; as a headline in a customized old-fashioned newspaper. It takes a bit of creativity and effort to do this—and of course it's completely unnecessary—but it's a lot of fun and adds to the specialness of the occasion. Besides, when it's all over and you're looking back over those response cards, it's amusing to see the lengths people went to to make you smile.

Addressing the Invitations

Depending on your sense of formality, it is perfectly acceptable to address your invitations to "Mr. & Mrs. Berchman," or simply to "Paul and Karen Berchman." If their offspring are invited, it's your choice whether to write "Dr. & Mrs. Kalfus and Family" or "Denis & Jane Kalfus," then on the next line, "Lisa and Robert." If a child being invited with his/her family is also a friend of the Bar/Bat Mitzvah child, it's nice to send a separate invitation.

It's trendy for invitations to be hand-calligraphed by a professional, especially if they're formal. And it does look nice, but it's one of those extra expenses that really aren't necessary, especially if you're trying to cut corners. You or someone with a neat handwriting can do it just as well. If you decide to address the invitations yourself, use a colored pen that matches the ink on the invitation.

The Great Stamp Hunt

Mea culpa: I did make myself crazy looking for just the exact right postage stamps (color *and* theme coordinated) to go on the invitations. I don't advocate it, because it's truly not necessary. But if you happen to be meshuga like me, here's how to go about it. First, have your invitation packet weighed so you know how much postage you will need. Then, start casing not only post offices, but those with philatelic centers. If you live in a big city and you have oodles of time, this is fairly easy to do. Take your invitation with you and peruse the stamp displays. Sometimes you will get lucky.

The theme of our son's Bar Mitzvah was the Olympics, and wouldn't you know, we found Olympics stamps. (Probably no one who got the invitation noticed, and our son couldn't have cared less, but *I* felt fulfilled.)

In our daughter's case, we didn't get so lucky. Even though I traipsed through every philatelic center in the five boroughs of New York City and through northern New Jersey (and made my poor husband do the same), I could not find any addressing her theme, carousel horses (actually, there *is* a stamp with carousel horses, but it was a collector's item and unavailable when we needed it). So we had to settle for color coordination only: her stamps ended up with pictures of killer whales and sea otters on them. She was less than amused. But at least they matched her selection of Sea Foam ink on the invitation.

A less time-consuming way to find the right stamp is to write to the United States Postal Service for their current philatelic catalogue, which features photographs of all the current stamps available to order. Their address: U.S. Postal Service, Philatelic Sales Division, Box 449997, Kansas City, MO 64144-9997.

A final note about mailing your precious invitations: when you go to the post office, ask to hand-cancel them yourself. Otherwise, you run the risk of the invitation being put through a machine and—after you've gone to so much trouble and expense to make it look gorgeous—having it arrive with those lines that make it look as if a truck ran over it.

Hidden Expenses

When ordering invitations out of a book, it may be possible to customize them, but remember that the more layers of paper you add, the more expensive they will become, as well as the heavier—which means extra postage. Any layer of material with shiny paper is going to cost more. So do custom colors and special typefaces.

Money-Saving Tips

Invitations is one area where you really can cut corners. Making your own is the first way; purchasing from a book, but at a discount, is another. Nearly every place that sells invitations gives discounts. Most stores will take off 10 to 15 percent; many people who sell privately out of their homes discount more: 20 to 25 percent.

But the best way to get a discount is to order the invitations through your temple. Then, no matter what you spend, you make the check out to the temple.

Those extra inserts I've been talking about cost money, if you can squeeze the reception information onto the invitation itself, do it. Directions cards can be written out by you and xeroxed: they don't need to be offset, just as long as they're readable.

Other Tips

Order thank-you notes at the same time. They can be a great deal simpler than the invitation itself.

If you're ordering from a book and customizing, but you're not completely sure about how the invitation will turn out, order one mock-up first. It will cost a few dollars, but if you hate it (or if the Bar Mitzvah child hates it), you can make changes while there's still time.

Before you order the biggest, most elaborate invitation ever, think about whether it will fit in most people's mailboxes: the most beautiful invitation, all bent and crushed, surely doesn't make the desired impression.

Mail out together invitations going to like groups of people (all the Florida relatives, all the kids) so one cousin won't think she was slighted when she hears from another cousin how beautiful your invitation is.

Expect to have to chase after "deadbeats" who don't respond by the time you've requested, or even soon afterward. Often the culprits are the kids and it may be your child's job to call and find out what's up. It's rude and it's a pain, but it's also a given.

Order more invitations than you need. You (or the calligrapher) *will* make mistakes, or you will suddenly think of another person or two you want to invite (certainly your child will). Most important, you *will* want an extra invitation or two for framing. It will be one of the most treasured keepsakes of the day.

Chapter Ten

A Little Bar Mitzvah Music, Please!

Whether or not music is part of the Bar/Bat Mitzvah celebration depends on the type of reception you're hosting and where it's being held. You may have rented the temple social hall, only to find out that music is not permitted on Saturday. Check your temple's policy if the reception will be held there. The same may go for some restaurants. Generally speaking, in a hotel or catering hall they pretty much expect that you will have musical entertainment.

The type of entertainment can be anything from a one-person band, to a folksinger to an Israeli dance troupe, all the way to a ten-piece band or a hotshot deejay with laser beams, smoke machines, and exotic dancers.

The music sets the tone for the party. If you want things low-key, think about one guitarist or pianist; if you wish to maintain the religious theme, there may be Israeli singers and dancers in your area who will add that flavor to your reception. However, if you're dreaming of kicking up your heels to the beat of "Celebration" or "I'm So Excited" (both of which have become Bar/Bat Mitzvah standards), you probably want major music. And since the star of the whole shebang is a thirteen-year-old, you just may find yourself in the middle of...

The Band vs. Deejay Debate

Your child: Deejays are better!
You: Nothing beats live music.
Child: Everyone has deejays!
You: I don't care what everyone has. Cousin Sharon had a band and it was wonderful.
Child: That's because they played *your* kind of music. Old stuff! Deejays play *our* music.
You: I'm sure a band will know all the current songs.
Child: Did you ever *hear* a Bar Mitzvah band play "You Can't Touch This"?
You: You have a point.
Child: Besides, it's *my* day, I should get my way. (Told ya' you were going to hear this one a lot).

In truth, there are pros and cons to both.

Bands do bring the cachet of live music, which many people find more exciting, immediate, and classy. Musicians who routinely play at Bar/Bat Mitzvahs tend to have a set formula of old standards and new favorites: they know there are at least three generations to please and they usually play a little something for everyone. A good band leader will know how to get people up on the dance floor and get down there himself, interacting with your crowd. Additionally, when some band members take a break, others can still be performing, which gives you continuous music.

There are problems inherent in having a band, however. Some are just too large for the room. They overpower the place *and* the crowd. A party of a hundred and twenty people does not need a ten-piece mini-orchestra. Many bands, however, will try and sell you extra musicians: if you really want a five-piece combo, but they generally play with six or more, that's what they will push for. Many don't feature the same musicians from week to week: you may have heard a wonderful six-member group, only to find that by the time of your party four of them are

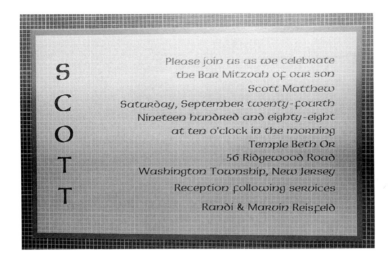

SCOTT

Please join us as we celebrate
the Bar Mitzvah of our son
Scott Matthew
Saturday, September twenty-fourth
Nineteen hundred and eighty-eight
at ten o'clock in the morning
Temple Beth Or
56 Ridgewood Road
Washington Township, New Jersey

Reception following services

Randi & Marvin Reisfeld

A typical invitation for a Bar Mitzvah is worded simply. (Photo by Randi Reisfeld)

Happy occasions when shared
by family and friends
become cherished memories

We invite you to join us
at the Bat Mitzvah of our daughter
Erica Michelle
Saturday, September twenty-eighth
Nineteen hundred and ninety-one
at ten o'clock in the morning
Temple Beth Or
Washington Township, New Jersey
Reception follows at Town and Country

Karen and Paul Berchman

A Bat Mitzvah invitation that is a bit more decorative. (Photo by Randi Reisfeld, courtesy Mr. & Mrs. Berchman)

A true original:
an invitation in a can!
(Photo by Randi Reisfeld)

An inventive way to RSVP.
(Photo by Randi Riesfeld)

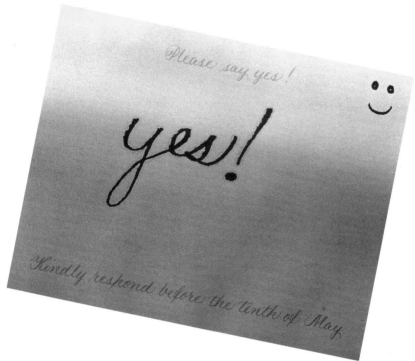

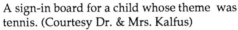

Be sure to code response cards. Some people—intentionally or absent-mindedly—will send them back without signing them.

A sign-in board for a child whose theme was tennis. (Courtesy Dr. & Mrs. Kalfus)

A photo collage of the children who are invited, at various stages of growing up, is a nice ice-breaker as the young guests try to find their pictures. The lyrics to "Forever Young" represented my own personal prayer for all the children. (Photo by Randi Reisfeld)

Decorating with balloons is festive and inexpensive. (Photos courtesy Mr. & Mrs. Reisfeld; Mr. & Mrs. Gardner)

Themes and favors: Giving each child a surfboard with his or her name on it established a beach theme *and* served as a seating card at the dais. (Photo courtesy Mr. & Mrs. Berchman)

At a tennis-themed party, the dais was called Center Court. Note the two handmade tennis players on either side of the sign. (Photos courtesy Dr. & Mrs. Kalfus)

PLAYBILL
Mitzvahpiece Theatre

An Evening with Jennifer
A One Woman Show

October 20, 1990

A "Playbill" created by the parents for a Bat Mitzvah whose theme was theater. (Photo courtesy Mr. & Mrs. Klein)

Not enough candles and too many people to be honored? Ask several to come up and be on the same candle. (Photo courtesy Mr. & Mrs. Reisfeld)

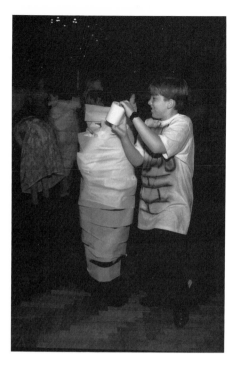

The mummy game is a favorite Bar/Bat Mitzvah event. (Photo courtesy Mr. & Mrs. Reisfeld)

A gift idea: A sculpture of a Bar/Bat Mitzvah on a slab of marble.

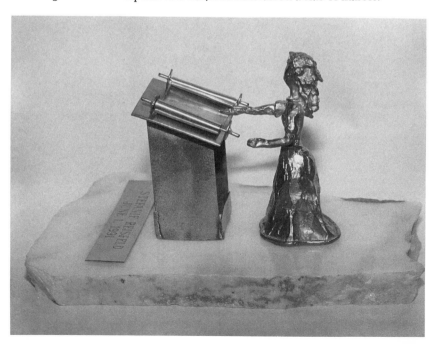

A nifty little gift to calm those Bat Mitzvah girl jitters (it also comes as a boy). (Photo by Randi Reisfeld)

Hello, BAT MITZVAH GIRL... I am your Personal Protector

will protect you against shaky hands, a squeaky voice, stomach butterflies, and forgetting all the Hebrew you ever knew. I guarantee a super party, exchangeable gifts, and a permanent feeling of pride. DON'T LOSE ME!

. . . and you will too! (Photo courtesy Randi Reisfeld)

no longer there. With a band, you can never be absolutely sure who will show up at your affair. You can, however, add a clause to your contract, naming specific band members you want on that day. That way, if they don't show up, you have a legitimate beef at bill-paying time.

Other complaints about a band: they don't always know the songs you want to hear, they often don't take requests, and they're not always familiar with the latest tunes—which usually doesn't bother the adults but will disappoint the kids. And even if the band does know the latest songs, the music can't possibly sound the way the kids are used to hearing it on the radio.

Bands also tend to be expensive. No matter where you live, it's doubtful you could get one for less than a thousand dollars.

It's a common misconception, however, that *deejays* are always less expensive than bands. There's a wider range of prices with a deejay, many *are* far cheaper than a thousand, but several, especially in cities like New York or Los Angeles, can charge as much as a band, sometimes more.

Kids like deejays because they can be assured of hearing the music they like, sounding the way they're used to hearing it. Deejays almost always take requests, and often come at least in pairs: while one is spinning the record, the other can be on the dance floor, entertaining the guests. Some are known for being real showmen, so you get a floor-show as well.

Deejays will often try to sell you a "complete entertainment package" (translation: you will spend much more money) including dancers—in our case, they were called "counselors" because their main function was to keep the kids occupied. It also includes games, paraphernalia (basketball hoops and the like), video screens, and special effects like fog machines and laser beams. Aside from the exorbitant cost, there are potential negatives about those package deals. For one thing, the deejay and entertainers can *become* the party. Instead of your guests being out on the dance floor celebrating, they're standing around (or worse, sitting) watching the deejay and sexy dancers do their thing. Personally, I don't think suggestive, scantily clad dancers—male or female—have any place at a Bar/Bat Mitzvah.

I have also seen at least one real damper put on a party by a high-priced deejay. When the fog machine (which the parents paid extra for, of course) went off, so did the smoke alarms and sprinklers. The entire Bat Mitzvah party, soaking wet, had to be evacuated from the hotel.

Both bands and deejays should know how to get your guests involved and should be able to sense when to switch gears if people aren't responding to the music. Both should play games and run contests with the kids. And most important, both should be able to work with the caterer in terms of the party's timing. When the caterer advises that a main course is being served, the band or deejay should switch to softer music so people can converse.

A *tip:* Bar/Bat Mitzvah parties work best when staggered, that is, when the children are served before the adults. In that way, you can dance to your favorite oldies while they eat. Then you can watch *them* playing games while you eat.

How do you resolve the great band vs. deejay debate? It helps to know your crowd. If you've invited many more adults than children, you might think more seriously about a band. If, however, you've invited adults who dance and are pretty hip to the latest music, a deejay may work just as well. Naturally, if you have a lot of kids to make happy, a deejay is probably your best bet.

Some people hire *both*. Those with megabucks and mega-crowds separate into two parties, with the youngsters and their deejay in one area and the adults and their band in another. Some bands, seeing the popularity of deejays soaring, will offer the alternative of bringing a deejay with them and charging you for the price of one extra musician. Who plays when is something that needs to be discussed beforehand.

Your ultimate decision, however, should be based on seeing your prospective musicians/deejays in action.

How to Hang Out, Uninvited, at Other People's Affairs So You Can Hear the Band

The easiest way to decide if you like a band or deejay is to watch them perform at another affair. Being a guest at another affair is, of course, the preferred way to do this, but not always possible. If you're in the position we were, and have not been to a Bar/Bat Mitzvah in twenty years, you have little alternative but to eavesdrop on other parties. (Of course, it's a good idea to let at least the band know you're coming.)

Asking around and compiling a list of good local bands or deejays with Bar/Bat Mitzvah experience is the first step. Calling to determine price, availability on your date, and overall friendliness (of course, at that point, they're all friendly and tell you anything you want to hear) and level of experience is next. Once the basic criteria are met, you really do need to see and hear them in action. Many will be glad to send you a videotape of themselves, or invite you to a showcase, but that isn't the same as seeing them at a party. If you insist, most bands or deejays will give you a short list of upcoming dates and places they'll be playing so you can check them out.

Which is exactly how we went about making our musical choice. For what seemed like months, we spent almost every Saturday night Bar/Bat Mitzvah hopping—standing outside ballrooms with our ears pressed to the door (well, okay, not pressed), hoping the doors would open frequently so we could glimpse the musicians in action. In order not to feel completely out of place, we dressed up, acted as if we belonged there, and figured most of the guests would just think we were relatives from the "other" side. Uncomfortable at times though it was, the system worked. Nearly all the band leaders came out to talk to us. We eliminated a lot of potential choices that way; what sounded terrific on the phone often sounded merely ordinary, or just plain terrible, in person.

However you make your choice, you should *do it early*. After deciding on the time, place, and format of your affair, this is really the next big decision on the docket. A year in advance is customary in certain areas with a big Jewish population—even more if you *must* have one particular deejay or band. No matter where you live, if the music is important to you, don't leave it till the last minute.

Musical Notes

Know what you're paying for. Before you sign any contract, read the small print. If you want continuous music, be sure to specify that and see that it's in the contract.

If you want music during the cocktail hour, see that that's included. Often, people want background music at that time, and one musician will do. Usually, it involves a small added charge.

If you're planning to have a large number of children, you may want to talk to your potential band leader or deejay about games. Do they play games with the kids, how many do they usually play, and what are they? If a lot of the children do not dance, you will want at least three or four games. If your Bar/Bat Mitzvah child has a favorite game, does the band know it? Who will supply the game paraphernalia? In our case, our daughter wanted the Mummy Game, which has to do with wrapping guests from head to toe in toilet paper (don't ask!). Since our deejay was unfamiliar with that particular diversion, we had to supply the Charmin. Which was no problem, since we knew about it in advance.

After you've signed on the dotted line, and given a deposit, make sure you know the terms under which it is refundable and when the balance is due. In most cases, you aren't required to pay in full until the last dance is danced. This is a good policy because it gives you some room to negotiate if you don't feel you've gotten what you contracted for.

Ask if your band leader or deejay plans to contact you before the party to go over specific songs you want played and to talk about the candle-lighting ceremony. The most experienced bands and deejays are helpful that way. They send you forms to list your musical selections, which helps you think the matter through clearly. If your band doesn't do that, you have to make your own timetable and contact *them*, especially if the specific songs to be played are important to you.

A week or so before the affair, get in touch with the band or deejay to go over the timing. The musicians should arrive at the party spot well before you get there to set up and confer with the caterer. Make sure you are specific about *when* the reception starts. I know of at least one case where the timing was altered a bit at the last moment and the band was never notified. The mother of the Bat Mitzvah spent the entire cocktail hour worrying about when the band was going to show up.

Personally, I leave little to chance. In addition to a letter going over the timing, I also sent a reminder about the child's name, our names (and the pronunciation of our names, because we were going to be introduced), the date of the affair, the place, the driving directions, who would be doing the *motzi,* the blessing over the challah, the name of our maitre d', and any other information I thought might come in handy. I xeroxed everything. Did I go overboard? Probably. Were there any mishaps with the music? No.

Should You Send a Song List?

Not if you really don't care all that much about the specific songs to be played and you trust your musicians to know what works and what doesn't. I, on the other hand, really do care. I spent months compiling lists of our favorite songs—slow romantic songs, fast dance songs, conga line songs, stroll songs, contemporary music the kids like, our best friends' wedding songs—constantly jotting down a good song whenever I heard it on the car radio (nearly causing a few accidents in the process). By the time our daughter's Bat Mitzvah rolled around, I had a ten-page list of songs.

None of which were played.

The point is, if there are a few songs you *must* have played, for instance, a mother/son or father/daughter dance, and more important, songs that the child being honored really wants, let the band leader or deejay know in advance. Overwhelming them with lists, however, rarely works. (My lists, notwithstanding, are fabulous and for sale at a reasonable price.)

Some Bar/Bat Mitzvah standards: "Celebration," "We Are Family," "Hot Hot Hot," "Conga," "Hands Up" (the Club Med song; it really gets everyone moving), "Wind Beneath My Wings" (has taken over from "Sunrise, Sunset" to top the schmaltz meter), "Shout," and the inevitable everyone-forms-a-circle-and-holds-hands-and-sways "That's What Friends Are For." You haven't lived until you've seen fifty 13-year-olds crushed together shouting out the words to "We Didn't Start the Fire" (they know them *all*) or "Ice, Ice Baby." (You also haven't lived until you've seen—as I have—the expression on rapper Vanilla Ice's face when told that his most famous song has become a Bar Mitzvah standard.)

Hidden Expenses and Money-Saving Tips

Feeding the Band. It came as a big surprise to us after our son's Bar Mitzvah when the caterer nonchalantly told us he'd fed the entire band and we now owed him an extra two hundred dollars. You don't have to supply lunch or dinner for the band members or deejay, but if you want to, know it ahead of time and work it out with the caterer.

Tax, Union Fees, and Overtime. Know in advance what these charges are. When applicable, they can seriously add up.

Band and Deejay Prizes. Talk about adding up! These are little tchatchkies—often shamelessly self-promoting ones—that the band provides to liven up the party. They may be wild hats, T-shirts, sunglasses, neon necklaces and earrings, loony over-size shoes, or other kinds of silly junk that kids (and adults) clamor for in the heat of the party. You pay for this junk. It will be presented as part of the package deal—usually just before the affair so you're in no state of mind to comparison shop or even think about whether you want it or not. And it's not necessarily that you don't want it, because it *does* add an element of fun and silliness, but you can save money if you provide your own prizes. Chapter 12 details some ideas for getting this stuff yourself for less money.

Chapter Eleven

Flowers, Balloons, Decorations, Oh, Boy!

This chapter is aptly named, because it could *put* you in Chapter 11!

You want your celebration to have a festive atmosphere, regardless of whether the reception is held in your own backyard or at the fanciest catering hall. Nothing creates the perfect mood like good decorations. In fact, decorations can end up being one of your major expenses—more than ten percent of your budget. There are ways to keep it in check, but this is an area where it's easy to go overboard.

In general, it's more work (and usually more money) to decorate at home or in a temple or a social hall, because you're starting from scratch, often with little more than the four bare walls. Restaurants, hotels, and catering halls are generally somewhat decorated already. Many even offer table flowers as part of their package deals.

But whether you spend a bundle or a pittance, this is one of the places where creativity, and even social consciousness, can best be expressed, and sometimes even triumph over cost.

Flowers and balloons are the most common decorative devices, but they are not the only way to go. For people to whom the religious symbolism is most meaningful, candles, menorahs (on Hanukkah, of course), and challah with embroidered covers have been used as centerpieces. A Bar Mitzvah family who wanted to use this opportunity to give to tzedakah placed a simple note in the middle of each table reading: "The money which would have been used to purchase flowers for this table has been donated by (the Bar/Bat Mitzvah child) in your honor to (a favorite charity.)" It's hard to argue that the spiritual meaning of the day is lost amid the celebrations when you see something like that.

Flowers

Flowers symbolize life, beauty, and renewal. They have decorated simchas like weddings and Bar and Bat Mitzvahs for ages. Most often used as centerpieces on each table, flowers can be fresh, dried, artificial, or silk. They can also be one of the most expensive ways to go about decorating, or the cheapest. Pricey florists are skilled at making up knock-your-socks-off arrangements featuring many different types of exquisite fresh or silk flowers. Less expensive alternatives include doing it yourself. If you are skilled at floral arrangement (or have a friend who is), you can go to a greenhouse, purchase flowers wholesale, in bulk, and make up your own centerpieces. One woman planted colorful geraniums in clay pots, painted original designs on each pot, and used them instead of flowers. The effect was lovely and unique.

If you are neither creative nor particularly original, and you want to use flowers, going to a recommended florist is your best bet for gathering ideas. A word of caution however: prices vary wildly and some florists will try to sell you more than you really need. You might find yourself thinking about flowers to decorate other parts of the room too. Potted plants, for example, placed in strategic spots are effective, if expensive.

Balloons

Balloons, nothing but a piece of rubber filled with air—well, helium—should be a cheap and colorful way to say, "Let's celebrate!" Often they are, but so many people have gone so far overboard that balloon artistry has become a small industry. Balloons can be used in a bouquet as a centerpiece; in double- and triple-rowed arches stretching over the dais or crisscrossed over the dance floor; with lights running through them; and even in super sizes that explode, releasing hundreds of smaller ones onto the dance floor. In other words, you can go crazy decorating with balloons and end up spending more than you might on fresh or even silk flowers.

Kids tend to like balloons better than flowers, however. Balloons come in all colors of the rainbow. And walking into a room filled with brightly colored balloons establishes a celebratory atmosphere right away—even if you haven't spent the equivalent of the Gross National Product on them.

To save money, you can rent a helium machine and blow them up yourself, or you can just keep your "balloonacy" within bounds: a few bouquets at the cocktail hour and a couple on the dais and on each table. Many people find an inexpensive way to decorate the entire room by hanging balloons from the ceiling. That can work, but if the ceiling is low, the strings hanging from them will be in everyone's face *and* in every photo.

A Word (or Two) about Flower or Balloon Centerpieces

Always have a sample made up first so you can decide if it's what you really want. Any reputable florist or balloon vendor will do that for you. Whatever you decide, try to mount your arrangement twelve to fifteen inches above the table, so people can see each other and conversation won't be blocked. (Of course, at some tables where the people aren't speaking to each other, low centerpieces might be just the thing!)

Many of your guests will want to take the centerpieces home. If you don't care who gets them, they will end up with whoever has the fastest hands. Problems may occur, however. People (often it's the kids) may argue over a centerpiece, or you may turn around to find that there's not even one left for you to take home. Making some sort of arrangement ahead of time is prudent. You could play the under-the-plate game: whoever finds a note, or a penny, or some marking under his or her plate gets the centerpiece. Or, whoever's birthday is closest to the date wins. You could attach a small, shiny star (or some cute sign) to each centerpiece, saying, "Reserved for Melissa," or whomever you designate.

Finally, you may elect to take several centerpieces (especially if they're floral arrangements) to a local nursing home or hospital, as a way of sharing your joy with those in less fortunate circumstances.

To Theme or Not to Theme—Is This the Question?

Many people hate the idea of themes. They think it takes away from the spiritual significance of the day. The Bar/Bat Mitzvah itself should be the theme; anything more is sacrilegious. If you feel that way, don't have a theme.

Personally, I think themes are fun, and I also don't think they necessarily take anything away from the meaning of the event. Rather, I think they can express not only what the day is about, but what the child is about.

Themes can demonstrate a social or religious consciousness, be a simple way to decorate the reception, express a particular interest of the child's, or just be an all-encompassing celebration of that child. Themes are endless in scope, limited not necessarily by your pocketbook but by your imagination and your sense of what is appropriate.

Some examples: The theme of a recent Bat Mitzvah was the child herself. Far from being crass and self-congratulatory, the theme allowed the family to introduce this child for who she is: a young person who cares about her world and the people in it. This girl asked every guest to bring an item of food to her Bat Mitzvah to feed the hungry. In the little newsletter her parents had printed up about her, she urged all the guests to work for peace and for the environment. The newsletter format allowed the parents and grandparents to express their pride and love publicly to the child. No way was this an expensive theme to carry out; in every way it was appropriate and meaningful.

In another case, the theme was the same—the Bar Mitzvah child—but the execution was completely different. Like the family just described, this one printed up a newsletter about their Bar Mitzvah boy, only it took the form of a popular sports magazine. It was titled "Jason Illustrated," and the articles and photographs were all in praise of Jason, starting with the birth and chronicling all his (mainly sports) achievements.

Was one of these themes significantly less meaningful than the other? It depends on your point of view. Jason's family was celebrating Jason. At what other point in his life are they going to be able to do that?

I have to be truthful here. Long before my daughter's Bat Mitzvah was even in the planning stages (it must have been before she was born) I heard about a Bat Mitzvah where the theme was "shopping." Each table represented a different trendy store, and each guest received a gift certificate from that store. At the time, I thought it was the most disgusting display of conspicuous consumption I'd ever heard of. At thirteen years old, the Bat Mitzvah's greatest interest is shopping! What a shonda! I was outraged. Until, that is, my daughter's affair began to take shape. Trying to figure out a theme based on her interests—well, shopping didn't seem quite so terrible after all. In fact, it seemed kind of. . . doable, if still not terribly appropriate. We didn't use it, but I am no longer so critical of what other people do.

Common themes revolve around sports (sometimes complemented by the personal appearance of a sports star, either out of season or on the disabled list—read: pots of money); computers; racing cars; cartoon characters; movie heroes; or rock 'n' roll. Games have been used as a theme, as have carousel horses, magic, a Western hoedown, a Caribbean island, Broadway, travel, and carnivals (complete with booths for games and tickets for prizes). Something simple like hearts or candy can be used very effectively. On the other end of the spectrum, on one occasion, a large room was transformed, into a jungle via rented trees with stuffed animals hanging from them. The theme, "It's a Small World," was executed as each guest received a "passport" seating card upon entering the reception. Each table was a different country and the dais was the airport.

Themes don't always have to be expensive to carry out. Here are two memorable ones that were high on creativity and relatively low on cost: A tennis theme was established simply by naming each table after a different tennis racquet company (Wilson, Prince, etc.). Seating cards were attached to a chocolate tennis racquet which the Bat Mitzvah's mom had made several months before and frozen. The centerpieces were tennis racquets made out of eucalyptus vine wrapped around cross-stitch, then attached in pairs and crisscrossed, anchoring balloon bouquets. The dais was center court.

In a family where the Bat Mitzvah is an aspiring actress, the theme was "An Evening With Jennifer—A One-Woman Show." Centerpieces were small director's chairs, each labeled with the name of a Broadway show. On each chair were props relevant to that show: a bottle of shampoo and a towel for *South Pacific,* a curly red wig and dog tag for *Annie.* Playbills were printed up, offering (phony and very funny) congratulations to the star from all the invited guests.

Thinking of themes can be fun—albeit all-consuming. At one point during the preparations for my daughter's party, I was helping her study for a science test. And suddenly I began to think, how about "Invertebrate" as a theme? We could have the crustacean table, the segmented worm table, the dais could be the centipede table...and I, of course, would not be happy unless I was seated at the slug table. You can measure just how crazy you're starting to get when thoughts like these begin to eat away at your brain.

Sign-in Boards

After the flowers have wilted and the balloons have burst, a sign-in board is a tangible keepsake for your Bar/Bat Mitzvah child. It can be very simple, made of Styrofoam, Lucite, or even mirrors, and usually bears the child's name, if not a photograph as well. Sign-in boards are routinely posted at the entrance to the reception, so all the guests can write their good wishes.

Sign-in boards can reflect your theme. Styrofoam cut into the shape of a giant guitar, decorated with a string of lights around it, works well for a music theme, for example. Or they can just be functional and decorative by themselves. Though many boards eventually end up relegated to the garage, some do hang proudly on the child's bedroom wall as a happy reminder of a special day.

Boudoir Baskets

Putting a basket of "necessaries" into the ladies' restroom is a classy touch. Florists will charge up to fifty or sixty dollars for it; however, it's better—and easy—to do yourself. Fill a small wicker basket with combs, brushes, hair spray, nailfiles, clear nail polish (to stop stocking runs), extra stockings, tampons, lipstick, band-aids, mascara—anything you can think of that someone might need during the party. Your female guests will be grateful.

Hidden Costs

When it comes to decorating, there are costly little booby traps everywhere. You're not dealing in per-person costs, and if you are impulsive and react to the ever more expensive cornucopia of goodies placed in front of you, it's easy to get carried away. Suddenly, what you thought was going to be a few hundred dollars' worth of balloons can escalate to a few thousand. Tread carefully and keep track of what you're spending. If necessary, give your co-planner veto power in this area.

Money-Saving Tips

- As a rule, balloons are cheaper than flowers.
- Making your own centerpieces is sure to save you a bundle.
- If you're in a place where it's offered, use the house flowers—or at least make sure you get an allowance toward your own centerpieces in lieu of theirs.
- If you are hiring someone else to do the decorating for you, think about creative types who are not yet established. They may do a fabulous job, and will cost a lot less.
- Before you hire someone to decorate your party, however, check with the place where you are having it. Some require that any decorators be heavily insured, and many nonprofessionals are not.

Chapter Twelve

Extras: Entertainment and Favors

"You mean we have to do something else?"

You've picked the place, dealt with decorations, decided on a deejay. What more could there be to do? Are you kidding? There are always more ways to spend money. One of them is opting for extra entertainment. Under this broad banner falls everything from a caricaturist to a full-blown carnival, with umpteen possibilities in between.

All kidding aside, there *are* reasons hosts look to provide additional entertainment, beyond the desire to spend more money and stage a bigger blast. If the guest list includes a large number of teenagers and younger children, they may need to be kept occupied, especially during the cocktail hour or any time when there's little structure to the party. Otherwise, they may simply run wild. A sad commentary to be sure, but in certain areas all too true. The daughter of a TV producer told me that in her experience, Bar and Bat Mitzvahs are often held at the fanciest hotels in Los Angeles. Typically, the youngsters leave the party, run up and down the hotel halls, and bang on doors.

Another child, invited to a swank affair at New York's Waldorf-Astoria Hotel (where the hosts had spent at least $100,000) told his parents that the best part of the party was playing in the elevators. Young guests have been known to hang out in the bathrooms, invade other affairs, and in some cases even become destructive. In any case, the goal is for them to be part of the party, not apart from it. One solution is to provide an activity for them, or hire entertainers to, in effect, baby-sit. Another advantage of extra entertainment is that it gives youngsters who are shy, don't dance, or don't know anyone, something to do.

On the other hand, many hosts don't feel the need for any of this at all, and not solely for financial reasons. They feel that yet another form of entertainment fractionalizes the party, divides the energy of the guests, and is just plain distracting. They may not have invited many young guests, and want them to be dancing, participating in band-led games, and not hanging around a caricaturist. Indeed, if you have hired a band or a deejay who knows how to keep kids involved, then extra entertainment may not be necessary. Or you may want to assign it a limited role, such as at the cocktail hour. Of course, if your party is only to last a few hours, or being held at home, there's little reason for this extra expense.

If, however, additional entertainment is something you do want to consider, it's not hard to find. Get recommendations from caterers, florists, and especially musicians—and, of course, from other people who have used them. Look in the classified sections of magazines and under "Party" or "Entertainment" in the Yellow Pages. In many parts of the country the variety is limitless. Needless to say, expenses can run anywhere from relatively minor to quite major.

Magicians, mimes, face painters, fortune-tellers, clowns, chimps, celebrity look-alikes, or even the real thing (I wonder how much Madonna *would* charge to come to your child's Bar Mitzvah?) are popular forms of amusement at parties. So are full-fledged carnivals (with booths, cotton candy, games, and prizes) and even professional fantasy troupes who actually stage a costumed, and sometimes even customized, revue for you. (We're now into major bucks.)

Professional *tummlers*—entertainers paid to mix with the crowd—may include dancers (your big chance to learn the Electric Slide!), as well as actors, singers, even acrobats.

Sometimes the objective is not only extra entertainment, but to provide a favor, a small take-home gift, at the same time. Since most hosts do give out favors for the youngsters anyway, this is seen as an ideal way to accomplish twin goals.

One souvenir for the kids to take home is caricatures of themselves, on paper or on a T-shirt, drawn by a professional artist. Photoimaging has become very popular: an instant computerized image of the child is superimposed onto magazine covers, baseball cards, mugs, key chains, buttons, or posters (there are many possibilities here). Other variations of the same thing are photos of the young guests posed with cardboard cutouts of rock or sports stars in a paper frame, or dressed up as a favorite rock, sports, or movie star.

Some forms of take-home entertainment also provide an arts and crafts project, such as "spin art" (one begins to wonder here if you're running a Bar/Bat Mitzvah, or a day camp).

Renting a sound booth for the entirety of the party gives kids the chance to actually record themselves and take home an original audiotape. Some outfits can even send each youngster home with a customized video of themselves costumed and lip-synching to their favorite song.

Aside from the cost factor and your just not wanting to provide extra entertainment, there are a few other things to be wary of. Some entertainers may be quite inappropriate at a party that is ostensibly for the children. Scantily dressed women or Chippendale-style dancers—not to mention strippers or "flashers," both of which I have witnessed at Bar and Bat Mitzvahs—are to say the least in poor taste, as are suggestive skits. Clearly, you want people who are reputable and experienced in entertaining at Bar/Bat Mitzvahs.

Take-home entertainment can be a potential problem, especially when the children must stand on line in order to get their prizes. It's time-consuming, and takes them away from the party for longer than you might want. A simple solution is to provide the artist or photographer with a list of the young people's names and have him call a few at a time. Or give out tickets that they can redeem at a specified time. That way, they won't feel they have to stand on line or be left out.

If you're considering this type of entertainment, be sure you're made aware of any *hidden expenses* before you make a commitment. It typically involves your having to provide the props, be it audio/video cassettes, T-shirts, mugs, or buttons. Those can all add up!

And when you're quoted a price for extra services, make sure you know either how long the entertainer will stay (some charge on an hourly basis) or how many guests will be taken care of. For example, a photoimager may quote you a price of $250, but that only includes photos of thirty-five kids and you expect sixty-five. Will there be one prize per guest, or may they come back for more? Know the total price for your specific needs before you sign on the dotted line.

Of course, if you're looking to cut corners, the whole concept of extra entertainment is something that can easily be cut out. It can be fun, and can head off kid-related problems, but it is not, in any way, shape, or form, necessary.

Favors are another story. True, they're not necessary either, but most people in party situations do go in for them. And most children expect them. Which doesn't mean they have to be expensive: with a little thought, research, and creativity, favors can be a comparatively minor expense.

They can be anything from a goody bag filled with candy to a plush stuffed animal. As mentioned before, the favor can be a take-home from the extra entertainment, or something entirely separate. They can be useful, or simply goofy throwaways like sunglasses, crazy hats, and neon necklaces to wear at the party itself. They can be reflective of your theme (beach balls, towels, and Styrofoam surfboards, with the child's name stenciled on them, have all been used as favors with a beach theme) or have absolutely nothing to do with it. Favors can be used for dais seating: a colorful shopping bag with each child's name on it (and favor in it) can be placed one to a setting.

Favorite favors include picture frames, inscribed with a phrase like "Picture me at Dana's Bat Mitzvah, June 1, 1992"; license plates bearing the child's name; T-shirts listing the names of all the kids at "Jared's Bar Mitzvah, September 24, 1991"; sweatshirts, boxer shorts, socks, or hats; water bottles, calculators, stationery, or banks; candy-filled mugs, gumball machines, and even small cameras. Almost anything goes.

Some people don't stop with the kids; they provide small souvenirs for the adults as well. We put pairs of socks on each adult table (hoping everyone would kick off their high heels and dance—it worked) and, as a partial goof, earplugs at the tables where we expected complaints like "The music's too loud; we can't carry on a conversation." Other people have provided lottery tickets for each adult (with the only half-joking stipulation that winnings must be split with the Bar/Bat Mitzvah family) and sent home Saturday night revelers with a bag of bagels and a copy of the Sunday paper. A nice touch, but expensive.

Money-Saving Tips

Shopping for favors is fun if you're up for it, but those adorable little extras can really add up. Ways to save include packaging as much as possible by yourself. If you're keeping it simple and just giving candy in a shopping bag or mug, it will keep costs down if you fill them yourself and wrap them up with a pretty ribbon.

Actually, making favors yourself works if you are talented in that area. It *can* be a fun family project.

Ordering from catalogues can be a great money saver. There are companies that usually sell to retailers but will also sell to you if you're ordering enough (which can sometimes be only a few dozen items). If you plan to buy in bulk, a company called Oriental Trading in Omaha, Nebraska, offers all kinds of novelties, from sunglasses to kids' watches, art supplies, even sporty radios, pens, pencils, and jewelry, at reasonable prices. The address for their catalogues is Oriental Trading Company, 4206 South 108th Street, Omaha, NE 68137-1215. Many other companies will allow you to order for their wholesale price, but most require a resale number that proves you are truly a retailer.

You may be able to order for the wholesale price just by calling up a particular manufacturer. The people who gave out cameras at their daughter's Bat Mitzvah did so by calling the company directly, and telling them they needed fifty cameras; they got the wholesale price.

For that matter, local merchants may be willing to give you a sizable break for ordering in bulk.

Home and school organizations are good sources for finding out about catalogues that feature fun kid stuff for good prices.

Don't overlook flea markets when shopping around. You may find a favor that is both original and affordable.

Give it some thought beforehand, and chances are you will come up with your own creative, less costly favor-saver.

Chapter Thirteen

Photos and Videos

When the day is done and the party's over, your most precious memories are of course carried in your heart. Most of us, however, like to carry a little reminder in our wallets too (after all, something has to replace the money that used to be there, before the Bar/Bat Mitzvah), as well as on our walls, coffee tables, and office desks. For this, we look to photographs, and for that, we look to a photographer.

Finding someone to photograph the Bar/Bat Mitzvah is a relatively simple affair. Finding the *right* someone could take a little time and energy—but what, at this point, doesn't? An immediate thrifty little thought might be to ask a friend, especially if you know an accomplished shutterbug who's already offered, or done it for someone else. It's a fine idea, but a friend who should be a guest is suddenly being asked to work, and may not be able to relax and enjoy the day. And if for some reason you're not happy with the results, it could put a strain on the friendship. Personally, I think it's great to have a friend as a backup photographer if someone has offered; but if having a quality pictorial memento of this day is important to you, go with a pro.

Start with recommendations from friends and especially caterers (these guys have seen everything). Look at newspaper ads and in the telephone directory, then shop around. Before you start making appointments for potential photographers to come to your home and display their wares (and give you their speil) know what you want. Compare apples with apples and know what you're getting.

Here's a partial list of what you should be looking for in a Bar/Bat Mitzvah photographer:

Someone with Bar/Bat Mitzvah Savvy. You want someone who's done this before, who knows when an important moment is coming up (the candle lighting, the challah, the hora) so you don't have to keep telling him or her. Otherwise, you run the risk of losing that all-important shot of you with your mouth wide open, screaming "Put me down!" when you're hoisted up on the chair.

Someone with Kid Smarts. The photographer is going to be working with the children, and it helps to have someone who is patient and knows how to coerce them into cooperating.

Someone Cooperative, with a good personality and demeanor, who will blend in with the party, do what *you* want, and not try to run the party to his/her convenience.

Someone with Up-to-date, Easily Checkable References. Call people who have used the photographer before and ask if they were satisfied and what, if any, problems they had with him/her.

Quality of the Work. This is the key point, though some people (me, again) are more finicky than others. The photographer should be showing you his or her best work. Ask yourself the following:

Are there shadows behind his subjects' heads? There shouldn't be. A pro brings devices, like an umbrella, to bounce light off and counteract shadows.

Are people posed with flowerpots on their heads? No, not really, but if the subjects aren't posed properly, whatever is in the background of the picture can look as if it's "sitting" on his/her head.

What backgrounds does he or she use? Are distractions moved

out of the way? Better yet, does he/she routinely bring professional backdrops?

Are the photos clear and in focus?

How are they cropped? Do you see more of the room than the subject?

Is this person amenable to outdoor shots, using available light?

Has he/she retouched the shots of people wearing glasses? Often there is an unavoidable glare, and a good professional will have them retouched for you. Same goes for the "red-eye"—you don't want to see that in your photos.

When taking candids, has the photographer gotten in the middle of the action and captured the moment?

The work's *creativity*. Don't expect miracles. You know that no photographer on earth, no matter how creative, is going to turn you into Christie Brinkley, but you want to be photographed in the most flattering way possible. Most of us don't want to look *too* posed and unnatural.

Has this photographer come up with any creativity in shooting other people? Something so insignificant as using the family pooch in the photo may give you an idea. Something about the samples you are being shown should turn you on.

Getting the Photos You Want

Once you have an idea of what the photographer offers, you should have a very clear idea of what you want. There are a few choices to explore. Do you want: just the proofs to keep and make your own album? Or would you prefer a leatherbound professional album? More posed shots than candids, or the other way around?

You should also think about—and discuss with the photographer beforehand—any particular pictures you want. Photographing the actual Bar/Bat Mitzvah ceremony is usually not allowed by most temples; however, you may be able to get shots at the bimah and with a prayerbook (if not the Torah) before or after the ceremony. If this is important to you, make sure you inform the photographer. Aside from the immediate family, you will no doubt want certain family groupings: grandparents, all the cousins, aunts and uncles, perhaps groups of friends. Make a list beforehand, letting the photographer know who the important people are, then designate one family member to round everyone up at a specified time.

No doubt you will want a shot of all the Bar/Bat Mitzvah child's friends. Find out when and where the photographer usually takes it. It may be easier to line all the children up on a stairway, or pose them all outside (weather permitting) under a tree or in a gazebo. This photo is potentially most important to the Bar/Bat Mitzvah child.

You will also want a record of certain moments during the reception, such as the candle-lighting ceremony, and presumably all the tables. Make sure the photographer routinely takes *two* shots of each: if you're making an album, you'll have a choice. Remind the photographer too, that in taking the table shots it's a nice idea to move people slightly away from the table; how many shots of half-eaten food do you want in your album?

If there are any other shots you want—for example of the room, all decorated before people come in—the photographer must be made aware of that too. If the photographer is not amenable to what you want covered, he or she may not be the right person for you.

Timing is another point to go over before you select a photographer. If you are planning posed formals of your immediate family (and perhaps grandparents too), when will they be taken? The best time is at least a day or two before the ceremony, even though it means getting dressed, coiffed, and made up one extra time. That way, the family will not be as rushed and nervous as you are bound to be on the big day. More important, you won't have to take time away from your guests to stand and pose for photographs. Find out if the person you are considering charges extra to come another day for the family photos. Some do; many do not.

Know What You're Getting

Before you make a final decision, be sure you know exactly what you are getting so you can compare one photographer with the next. Here are some questions you might want to ask:

- Is there a separate fee for photographing the affair, and another one for the album? What is the usual price range?
- How many proofs can I expect to get? (For a four-hour affair, it should be several hundred).
- Do I automatically get to keep all the proofs? Or is there a charge?
- Can I keep the negatives?
- Will the same photographer who takes the posed formals actually be at the reception the entire time? (You don't want to learn that the accomplished photographer you're about to hire plans to send an assistant instead.)
- In terms of the album: how many shots will I get for the fee quoted? (Many photographers will only give you thirty; others, thirty-six for the same price; still others, forty.)
- How much extra for each photo beyond those included in the set fee?
- How much extra for more than one photo on a page?
- How much extra for a full-bleed centerfold?
- Is there a set fee for grandparents' albums? How much is it and what are they entitled to within that fee?
- Do I have the option of not making up a formal album? What is that charge?
- Does the photographer offer a package deal? If so, for a set fee do I get extra photos besides the album, that is, several wallet-sized shots, an 8 × 10 or 11 × 14 for framing?

If you are aware of all these costs beforehand, there can be few hidden expenses. There are a few ways to save money in this area, however.

- Choose someone who is just starting out. If you find a photographer who meets the other criteria, but is perhaps not very well known, the cost may be a whole lot lower and it may be worth the gamble.

- If you do choose a free-lancer (or someone just starting out), ask if you can buy the film and have it developed yourself. That way, you get to keep the negatives. If you make up your own photos it will cost a lot less than having it done by the photographer.

- It's a good idea to keep the proofs if you can. Then you can compile your own grandparents' albums and possibly save a few hundred dollars. Naturally, that also allows you to give certain pictures to friends without having to pay extra for them.

Video Smarts

Gaining in popularity—in some circles, outdistancing the tried-and-true, still-and-staid photographs—is a video souvenir of the Bar/Bat Mitzvah. An instantly gratifying replay of the day, videos capture the moment and allow you to relive the day's highlights time and again. (Or be embarrassed by your antics time and again, as they are forever captured on tape. And I found they don't change, no matter how many times you view them!)

Often, the still photographer you hire will offer video service too. It might be advantageous to book both as a package; they'll probably work together smoothly and between them, capture everything you want. The disadvantage may be the price. It may be more practical to hire a separate, less expensive video person. Shop around. Ask to see samples of friends' videos. (They will be only too glad to show them.) You might consider using a handy friend, but again, that friend is no longer a guest, but a worker. I actually found my video person at a Bar/Bat Mitzvah exposition in a hotel, where many professionals were displaying their services. Check the local papers.

Although it often isn't possible to shoot still photographs during the Bar/Bat Mitzvah service, many temples do allow the service to be videoed. That would truly be a significant keepsake. At some synagogues, the policy is to use their videographer only (sometimes, it's a fund-raiser); at others, you can bring your own.

Aside from the service, you will want to have the reception videoed. Commonly, a two-hour tape is made, which means your video person has to have the smarts to know when to shoot and what parts can be omitted. Because of this, you will want someone familiar with the format of Bar/Bat Mitzvah receptions. In any case, you will want to go over specifics, as you would with the photographer.

Some things you should be asking when considering a videographer:

- Will he use a rolling cart or simply balance the camera on a shoulder? Many people find a cart preferable, since no one can be completely steady.
- What will the lighting situation be? People don't want glaring video lights in their face during a party.
- Will cables be dragged around on the floor? (Most videoers know better, but check.)
- Will he/she stay for the entire party? You might not want the closing moments missed.
- Does the person do special effects (freeze frame, divided frames, etc.) and is there an extra charge for them?
- Is the price quoted for an unedited tape? What's the difference and how much more would it be for an edited version?

- Will you take the video home with you that night, or have to wait for it? How long?
- And when is the final payment due?

Get everything in writing, exactly as you want it, before signing a contract and putting down a deposit.

Video interviews have become popular, that is, the video person approaching guests, asking them to tape messages to the Bar/Bat Mitzvah child. Most people have strong opinions about video interviews, ranging from "They're the most touching souvenir we have" to "They should be banned." It depends partly on whether you're the host or the guest: Hosts generally like to see what other people say to their child; guests usually hate a microphone stuck in their face as they are chomping on an hors d'oeuvre. If you don't want interviews done at all, make sure your video person knows this. If you do, direct him/her to ask people first, before turning the tape on, if they would like to say something for posterity. Letting your guests compose themselves and think of something to say is the best way to go. For the record, most people say basically the same thing: "We're so proud of you. You did a wonderful job!" In truth, it's the younger guests who are the most imaginative: Instruct your video person to get *them* on tape; those will be the memories most precious to your own youngster.

Other directions you might want to give your videoer involve capturing the candle lighting, the hora, the motzi over the challah, and some of the dancing.

Of course, the videoer will need to know who the closest family members are, to train the camera on them; it's best to send a list ahead of time (I included what they would be wearing and what they look like, to help the person figure it out).

Many video people ask for a series of still photos of the child growing up, to start the video, as well as a favorite song ("Forever Young" tops the charts in this category).

Do you really need both, a photographer and video person? Will you ever look at the video beyond the first couple of times? Will an album of photos be stashed away and rarely retrieved for perusal? Only you can answer those questions. There's no question that if you opt for both, the expense can be tremendous. In general, a professional leatherbound album of photos is more expensive than a video. But you don't need a TV and VCR around in order to enjoy it.

Either way you go, always remember to send a written reminder to the person(s) you hire a week or two before the big day with the pertinent details: name of your child, date, place, and driving directions, and the time they should be there and ready to shoot. If you haven't done it in prior meetings, this is the time to include lists of family names and descriptions, plus any specific pictures you want and other directions you have. The less you leave to chance and assumption, the more enjoyable your keepsakes will be.

Chapter Fourteen

The Great Seating Plan

Where guests sit at the reception should be a fairly easy part of the planning, right? Let's put it this way: organizing the strategy behind the Gulf War was probably simpler.

Do you really need a seating plan? Nonassigned seating *is* more low-key and casual. But if you are having more than seventy-five guests, a seating plan is a good idea. It adds an element of formality you may not have wanted if you're planning, say, a buffet. But without one, you run the risk of people walking around carrying food, not knowing where to sit. Or you end up with people who know each other crowding around one table, while the few who don't know anyone sit stranded by themselves. Besides, not having a seating plan takes away some of that much-needed aggravation you have become so accustomed to by now!

Part of how you go about arranging the seating will depend on the number of people at each table. Some caterers have rules about this—no fewer than ten, no more than twelve—which can make the task even harder than it needs to be. Most caterers will give you guidelines rather than rules, for instance, fewer than eight at a table looks bare, more than twelve can be crowded. However, if you need to create one or two larger tables, most caterers will accommodate you.

Along with figuring out how many people per table, it's a good idea to get a layout of the room itself and find out (or decide yourself) where the tables are placed: where they are in relation to each other, to the dais, to the buffet, if you're having one, and, most important, to the music. That will help in deciding where to put people. A general rule is that the oldest generation prefers to sit as far as possible from the source of the music and as close as possible to the buffet. The kids, on the other hand, should be put near the music. Knowing where the tables are situated also helps when you're trying to put family members or friends fairly close together.

Seating the Adults

Okay, now the fun part. Who sits with whom? The first, most obvious task is to put friends who know each other together, then like relatives—your cousins, your spouse's cousins, and so forth. Then your friends, neighbors, and business associates. It sounds logical, but it never works out that neatly. There will always be too few at one table and too many at another. When you try to break up one large table, chances are there won't be enough people to fill two. A solution is to combine two small groups, such as four old friends with six people from the office.

A feuding family, however, takes a bit more planning, for instance, if ex-spouses are not on speaking terms, or simply a case where Aunt Hilda doesn't speak to Cousin Shaynela. Certainly, if divorced couples are not on friendly terms you would try to separate them. But when some relatives just don't get along and there is no way to keep them apart, they might end up at the same table. Not to agonize over it: they are adults and they will find a way to cope. (They don't have to sit right next to each other.) However, be careful about putting smokers and vehement antismokers together: you don't want fist fights to break out! And of course you will have invited some people who don't know anyone else at all.

So you start to mix and match, like shuffling a deck of cards, with the goal being for everyone to be comfortable at their assigned table. Most hosts try to seat guests at a table where they know at least one other person, or barring that, with outgoing, friendly people who will initiate conversation. Or, if the guest breakdown warrants it, you can put all the people who don't know anyone else together—"a table of strays," as one host tagged it. At least they have that much in common, and you can introduce them to each other beforehand. Some put all the singles together at one table, regardless of their relationship to the host family. Sometimes this works out, but it makes many singles uncomfortable.

One woman solved the problem of making everyone comfortable by printing up and distributing a Guest Guide. Along with a brief description of each guest, she noted their interests and at which table they would be seated. It proved a terrific icebreaker as people sought each other out.

Naturally, you do your best to make everyone happy, but in the long run it pays to remember that no one is nailed to his or her chair. If people aren't satisfied with the table to which they're assigned, between courses they can get up and move, shmooze with whomever they want.

Where Do *You* Sit

A good question. With your relatives or your spouse's? With friends? Which ones? Many hosts put themselves at the "strays" table, as the best way to make those people feel comfortable. But if you do that, you often aren't with the people closest to you. It's a very personal decision, often based more on the expectations of family and friends than on whom you would really like to be with. One thing to remember when you are toughing this one out: in all probability you will not be sitting much at all. As hosts, you will be mingling, flitting from one table to the next. It's doubtful you will be stationary long enough to even eat. So in that sense, it hardly matters where you sit. If it means that much to your parents, place yourself with them; if you think it will make "strays" that much more comfortable, sit there.

We compromised by breaking our friends up into separate tables, mixing the strays in with them, and putting ourselves at one of those tables. I did hear of one couple who put placecards for themselves at every table, and spent the reception rotating. We did not go that far, but did pose with each table as they were being photographed.

Children's Seating

The guest of honor—the Bar/Bat Mitzvah—usually sits among friends, either at a long dais or at individual tables, like the adults. Although some believe that if the youngsters are seated at tables like adults they will act more grown-up, this is really a decision most people leave to the Bar/Bat Mitzvah. Some come up with a combination: a teen table for those significantly older than thirteen and a tot table for those much younger, while school and camp mates sit at the main dais along with the Bar/Bat Mitzvah.

The setup of the dais really depends on how many kids you are having. One common configuration is the barbell shape: two long rectangular tables with round tables on either end, plus one round one in the middle for the Bar/Bat Mitzvah and his or her two closest friends. This type can accommodate forty kids easily. Another frequently used setup is the E-shaped dais, featuring several long rectangular tables with three or four more "arms" abutting them perpendicularly. This shape, too, can accommodate forty or more children. Ask the caterer which configuration has worked best in the room previously. Or, if you are doing this yourself, ask the Bar/Bat Mitzvah for a preference.

My daughter preferred the barbell—it made it easier for her to decide on the seating. She placed herself and two best friends in the middle and had camp and Hebrew school friends on one side of her, school chums on the other. She put all the boys from school at a round table on one end, all her cousins at the other end.

The basic concept in seating the children is the same as it is for the adults. Try to seat them near someone they know. If they won't know anyone there, seat them near a friendly, talkative soul. Most Bar/Bat Mitzvahs will want to handle this themselves. Let them; it's one less thing for you to do!

Techniques

You can make lists till you're blue in the face, crossing out names, placing them here, moving them there, until you have used up entire legal pads. There are easier ways. The best is probably index cards, especially if you have already set up a guest list system that way. For seating purposes, on each card put the name of a couple (if they're sitting together) or a single. Lay the cards out on a flat surface and start placing people around imaginary tables. That way, you will have them all in front of you at once and can make as many changes as you want with a clear overview at all times.

Another possibility is to use the RSVP cards and shuffle them around. The only problem with this method is when families have RSVP'd together but the children won't be sitting with the adults. You will have to make up separate cards for them. Computer-savvy Bar/Bat Mitzvah planners can create labels from the database of guests, print them out, and shuffle accordingly. Or you can do what we did: wrote names on pieces of paper and cut them up, and moved them around like players on a chessboard. At one point I got so frustrated, I just threw them all up in the air and decided that wherever they fell, that's where people were going to sit!

When you are satisfied with the tables—or as satisfied as you will ever be—make a master list of who is at which table and the total number of people at each. Xerox this list; keep one copy for yourself and give one to the caterer who will need it for place settings.

Seating Cards

Once you know who is going where, you will need seating cards or placecards which the guests will pick up on their way into the reception. (Youngsters' seating cards are generally placed on the dais, right at their seats.) This should not be a major expense, especially if you are having the reception at a place where the caterer provides them. All you then have to do is fill in the guests' names and table numbers. You could have the cards calligraphied, but that's another expense which you may deem unnecessary. If the caterer doesn't provide them, or if you are the caterer, you can pick up inexpensive seating cards at any party supply or stationery store. You might want to match the color to your color scheme, or just get plain white.

If you want to be different, or have the seating cards reflect your theme, there are myriad ways to go about it. Tickets bearing the guest's name and table are often used with a sports or theater theme; one hockey fanatic had Lucite pucks made up for this purpose. At a Disney-themed affair, the seating cards were little Mickey and Minnie key chains attached to a card. Others have used mini shopping bags with cards in them, cassette tapes, or chocolate molds of the theme (tennis racquets, carousel horses). One really creative family used old snapshots of the guests themselves attached to a card with only the table number on it. What an icebreaker that was!

Whatever you decide to use as table cards, *always order extras*. (You will lose some, the calligrapher will goof, there will be last-minute table changes because of cancellations and the like.) Be sure to alphabetize the cards as soon as you are finished filling in the info. When they are placed that way on a table at the door, it will be easier for guests to find theirs.

Table Tips

- If you have a theme, name the tables instead of numbering them. It can be creative and fun. For a theater theme, people have used the names of plays; for sports, the names of teams; for travel, the names of cities. A camp theme gave each table the name of an activity; an Olympics theme named each table after an event. Use your imagination, and that of the Bar/Bat Mitzvah person.
- Xerox every list and table configuration and give the caterer and decorator copies as requested. If there are last-minute changes, they can be dealt with.
- If this is not your first Bar/Bat Mitzvah, you may find it helpful to go back and look through table arrangements for your previous reception. Conversely, if this is your first, keep copies of everything you have done, to make the next time easier.
- The most important tip of all: don't reveal your seating plan to anyone before the reception. If you do, you are inviting complaints and lots of extra aggravation. There's no way you will please everyone, but you don't have to know about it beforehand.

Chapter Fifteen

The Candle-Lighting Crew

"Grandma Estelle,/You are so much fun,/Please come and light/Candle number one ...."

No one quite knows just how the candle-lighting ceremony, so crucial to Bar and Bat Mitzvahs as we know them, originated. While there is documentation aplenty for the Torah readings and blessings, the seudat mitzvah meal, and even music and celebration, nowhere in historical writings about Bar Mitzvahs is any mention made of the candle-lighting. Needless to say, the rhymes that go with them are fairly new too. It probably started a few decades back in the USA, as an acknowledgment of the child's birthday and to bestow good wishes upon him or her.

Yet we do it; even those who choose to dispense with the more materialistic aspects of the Bar/Bat Mitzvah ceremony would not consider getting rid of the candle-lighting ritual. Even if we don't understand the historical significance, if any, we can attest to its powerful emotional appeal.

If you haven't done it before, be warned: the candle-lighting ceremony is very moving and when you see the people who mean the most to your child lighting a candle, it will be hard to remain dry-eyed. When the Grandma who rocked him as a crying infant bends over to give him a kiss in front of everyone, when the friend who watched her every day after school lights a candle and gives her a hug, it can't help but move you in a very elemental way. That is when you realize the depth of human kindness and breadth of history you have with these people and the love that surrounds you and the child at this moment. And if that isn't what the whole thing is about, I don't know what is. The moment your own immediate family is called to light a candle becomes one of those you cherish in your heart forever. And if all goes well, on film and videotape too!

The candle-lighting ceremony is most often held following the service. If there is a reception, the most common time is after the cocktail hour and just before the meal and the dancing begin. Traditionally, it is followed by a lively hora, the circle dance in the course of which your friends hoist the Bar/Bat Mitzvah person and his/her family up on those wobbly chairs which you're sure you're going to slip off of, to your embarrassment. (Actually, there's more chance you'll be embarrassed weeks later when you see the photographs and realize you didn't cross your legs and your dress rode up. A tip: if you're wearing a short dress, cross your legs at the ankles.)

Although thirteen candles is theoretically the norm, many people have gone beyond that—to fifteen, sixteen, even seventeen candles. They don't want to leave out any of the important people. That's reasonable, but adding more than three or four extra candles will make for a very long candle-lighting.

Who Ya Gonna Call?

Choosing the people to be honored with the first few candles is usually a straightforward affair: grandparents of the Bar/Bat Mitzvah are almost always called up first; brothers, sisters, and parents of the child bring up the rear. It's those candles in the middle that can be tricky.

Aunts, uncles, and close cousins are often on the list, especially when they have a relationship with the Bar/Bat Mitzvah. So are great-aunts and great-uncles, even if those family ties are not the strongest. But the choices really are yours and the Bar/Bat Mitzvah's to make; there are no rules that must be followed except the ones you devise yourself. Some people call only relatives, thereby heading off any potential hurt feelings among this friend or that. Or only friends if there are no close relatives. I tried to call those people who have a history with my child. That made for a mix of family and friends, ours *and* our daughter's.

Naturally, the Bar/Bat Mitzvah will want to honor his or her friends as well. If you thought it was hard narrowing down your own choices, wait till you try reasoning with your child. "But Mark's my best friend!" "But Melissa's my other best friend!" "But they're all my *camp* friends!" "But he called me." "But I promised . . . " and so on. In cases where the number of children who "must" light a candle is just too large, there are solutions. One friend can light a candle representing all the friends. One from each group (camp friends, Hebrew school friends) can do it. Or, as has been done, the entire dais can troop up to be on one candle—a crowded candle to be sure, but that does take care of the group photograph at the same time, and no one's insulted.

Grouping people together, in fact, is not a bad solution when there are too many adults you'd like to honor but don't want the candle-lighting to go on forever. As long as the important people are up there, lighting a candle, does it matter if they are not alone? You do run the risk of insulting one or two who felt they deserved their own candle, but (and this is precisely why this phrase is oft repeated) you can't please everyone. Besides, it is my experience that people who are easily insulted about this stuff have not had to give a Bar/Bat Mitzvah. When they do, they will either understand or take revenge!

The candle-lighting, however, can be a time to honor people you could not give an aliyah to. In Orthodox temples, women may not have aliyot, but nothing stops you from giving all the significant women in your child's life a candle.

There are also ways to include each one of your guests in the candle-lighting ceremony, without calling each one up individually. Some hosts have put a candle at each table, or one at each place setting, and during the ceremony, called upon everyone to light one. That way, no one could feel slighted or left out. Or, if you feel strongly that the ceremony should represent more than just your family, you might ask each guest to observe a moment of silence and then to light a candle for Soviet Jewry or for the hungry or for Jews who are suffering anywhere in the world. There are opportunities for making the moment significant and meaningful and the candle-lighting is certainly one of them.

Another way of handling the candling: thirteen candles on the cake, each representing a good wish—health, happiness, prosperity, peace—instead of a person.

If you choose, the candle-lighting can be illustrative of your theme as well. At an affair where the theme was show business—the child was talented and theatrically oriented— instead of candles the Bat Mitzvah, whose name was Jennifer, gave out "Jennies," little statuettes that resembled Oscars. Important people were called up to receive one: for a stepmother, "Best Adaptation of an Original Play"; for a much married sister, "Best Sequel to the Original." Did the ceremony lose its significance? Not really. In a broader sense it represented this child and her family. Was it clever? Absolutely. Was it fun for the child and parents to dream up? You'd better believe it.

Working on the candle-lighting presentation can in fact be a family project, something fun to do together as part of your preparations. After you've collaborated with your child and husband in choosing who will be honored and how, the real fun begins ...

Candle-Lighting Rhymes

No way is it necessary to compose little rhymes when calling people up to light a candle. Either the child, or, in cases where the child is too shy, the deejay, bandleader, or caterer, can simply call the honorees' names and mention the relationship: for example "Grandma Alda," "Aunt Marion and Uncle Sol." But many Bar/Bat Mitzvahs chose a rhyme, an anecdote or, nowadays, even a rap to introduce the candle-lighting crew. Usually the introduction includes something significant about the child's relationship to the person ("Aunt Susan taught me how to bake,/Now come up and light the next candle on my cake," or, "Grandpa Jack takes me to ball games for fun,/Please come up and light candle number one"). Many rhymes are just plain funny ("My mom and dad are special to me,/They're paying for my whole party"); others have a little bite ("We share holiday meals with Uncle Pete and Aunt Kate,/To every one you always come late"). Many girls, especially, really get into this and come up with pretty creative intros.

If neither you nor your child is into it, however, but you want to do something creative, here's my suggestion: crib them from other people. People tend to save their candle-lighting rhymes and most are happy to share them. If you can get your hands on a few, surely you can find sayings that fit your own crew. Just substitute the names. What's the difference if it's Grandpa Leo or Grandpa Henry? No one will know the difference.

Rhyming works best when the Bar/Bat Mitzvah is the rhym-master. The best candle lighting I ever saw was done by a girl who created rap songs for each guest. Her exuberance and love for each person she called was so obvious and genuine, it truly touched everyone who was there.

Significant Songs

Along with creative introductions for each person come the songs. As each person makes his or her way up to the Bar/Bat Mitzvah child, the band can play a representative tune. This can be fun to plan—or agonizing, depending on your point of view. (You can also crib songs from other people: this is where networking pays off.) Here are some examples to get you started. For people who have traveled to the Bar/Bat Mitzvah, there is always an appropriate travel song ("Chicago," "Rocky Mountain High," "New York, New York," "California Dreamin'"). We played "Little Sister" when our son's sister came up, and "He Ain't Heavy, He's My Brother," when it was her brother's turn.

Some songs are funny. For a couple who are constantly bickering, you can play "Opposites Attract"; for bickering sisters, "She Drives Me Crazy." For grandparents, "Through the Years" or anything from *Fiddler on the Roof* is usually appropriate. If you come up totally blank, you can always rely on someone's wedding song if that works. The theme from *Perry Mason* or *L.A. Law* works for lawyers. "Girls Just Want to Have Fun" has worked for groups of a Bat Mitzvah's friends, and of course, every "friend" song ever written ("You've Got to Have Friends, "You're a Friend of Mine," "I Get By With a Little Help From My Friends," "That's What Friends Are For," and "Old Friends") have become candle-lighting standards.

Of course, when dreaming up these absolutely perfect songs for each person, be aware that only a first few bars will be played. The other thing to remember is that most of the guests will not realize which song is being played or what the significance is. But if *you* do, that's enough—especially if you're enjoying finding songs to fit. Driving to and from work, I would frantically jot down songs whenever they struck me as having any possibility of relating to a friend or relative.

The very last candle is usually reserved for the Bar/Bat Mitzvah person—with the appropriate song, of course, being "Happy Birthday."

Candle-Lighting Tips

- Make a list of who is coming up and in what order, plus the song to be played for each. Make several xerox copies and give one to the band leader or deejay and another to the caterer. It is the caterer who will be handing the candles to the Bar/Bat Mitzvah and will want to know how many are needed.
- Write out the candle-lighting rhymes or intros and xerox them. Give one copy to the caterer and one to a friend to

hold, just in case you forget to bring your copy with you for the crucial moment!

- If the intros are being handled by the bandleader or deejay, make sure they know the proper pronunciation of people's names. Write them down phonetically if necessary. Nothing's more irritating than having Uncle Saul introduced as "Sal," or "Susan" instead of Suzanne.
- A nice (but unnecessary) touch is giving a single rose to each woman as she lights a candle.
- Save all your rhymes and songs to pass along to the next person!

Chapter Sixteen

Alternatives

If everything you have read up to this point seems too much—too much work, too much expense, too time-consuming—or just doesn't suit your needs, take heart: there *are* alternatives to the traditional temple-to-reception routine. In fact, there really are no hard-and-fast rules for having a Bar or Bat Mitzvah. Anything is possible and almost anything is acceptable, as long as it works for your family and especially your child. You don't have to please anyone else and you don't have to justify your choices. Hopefully guests will accept your invitation because they want to share the joy of the simcha, not because they want to feast on a four-course dinner.

If you don't have the money to finance a big party, or just can't see spending that kind of money on this occasion, the trick is to find out what you do want in order to make the day meaningful. Perhaps you want food to be an element, but not music or lavish decorations. Perhaps you want food, background music, and some decorations, but not a lot of guests and none of the more obvious trappings of conspicuous consumption. Having the party at home, at a small restaurant, the temple, or a social hall could work well in this situation. You pick the elements you want and nothing more.

If money is not the problem, but you want to emphasize the religious significance of the day, perhaps you might consider hosting a Bar/Bat Mitzvah weekend at a religious retreat. No one would have to travel on the Sabbath and the intimacy couldn't be greater.

Naturally, there are other places you can take your guests for a weekend Bar/Bat Mitzvah getaway. Many resort hotels that cater to a largely Jewish clientele feature Bar/Bat Mitzvah package weekends. Ads are always found in Jewish newspapers or publications. Off-premises caterers are also a good source for finding weekend places.

Perhaps you don't want the formality of a temple for the service. Did you know that it's entirely possible to have your child become a Bar/Bat Mitzvah at home, or somewhere else of your choosing, without a rabbi present? Of course, you would need to design a curriculum for the child and hire someone learned to teach him or her. Several years' worth of work may need to go into it, but many people put that much energy into throwing a party.

If your child is reaching Bar/Bat Mitzvah age but hasn't been to Hebrew school, and you've just made the decision to have a Bar/Bat Mitzvah, there's no reason it can't be done quickly and meaningfully. There are tutors who will come to your home to teach your child, and temples that will perform the Bar/Bat Mitzvah service even though you are not affiliated. You may not have your pick of the day—it might have to be a Monday or a Thursday—but the goal will be met. And if you were thinking of a reception, but don't want it at home, there are always places willing to accommodate you, possibly on a weekday or a Sunday, or during a slow season.

If your child has a learning problem, or is disabled, he or she can still become a Bar/Bat Mitzvah. If you can't find a specific program in your area through the local temples or Jewish organizations, write to The Board of Jewish Education, 11710 Hunter's Lane, Rockville, MD 20852, or call (301) 984-4455. They may direct you to programs like the one run through the United Jewish Appeal Federation called Sh'ma V'ezer (Listen and Help).

A Party for the Kids

The most popular alternative to the traditional hoopla is simply to sponsor a lovely kiddush for your guests, and a for-kids-only party afterward or on another day. This option may solve a multitude of problems, for it does away with the major expenses, and also the major tsuris that sometimes accompanies this event—especially if you are divorced. (More on that a bit further on in this chapter.)

Parties that celebrate a child's Bar/Bat Mitzvah can really be held anywhere and with as many or as few of the extras as you want. There could be a deejay, there could be some balloons, you could hire a photographer and/or video person. Or you could skip any or all of the above, again depending on your needs.

Here are a few ideas for a children's-only party that have worked splendidly for people.

A *Swim Party*. It was held in a hotel's indoor pool. The kids snacked, played games, and jumped in and out of the water—and had a ball. There were a few adults, immediate family and friends, who were served drinks and hors d'oeuvres in this very informal setting.

A *Disco Party*. Many nightclubs will rent out space and all their facilities during the *day* for a kids' dance party. You get the house deejay, all the latest music, maybe even the video screens, and fast, simple food for several hours. Depending on the setup of the club, some adults may feel comfortable as well.

A *Pizza and Music Party*. Renting a rec room or social hall and bringing in your own deejay, decorations, and balloons can be a fun way for a young teenager to celebrate his/her Bar/Bat Mitzvah with friends. A very inexpensive way to go, and one that will no doubt satisfy the kids completely.

A *Tennis Party*. Many tennis or fitness clubs are available for parties. If this is something your child is interested in, it might fit into those Bar/Bat Mitzvah plans quite well. You would probably have to bring the food.

A *Roller-skating or Ice-skating Party*. Similarly, neighborhood rinks may have party packages, including deejay and food.

A *Sing-along Party*. Sing-along clubs are opening all over the country; they're a lot of fun and work especially well for parties. Background music for the latest songs and a video screen with lyrics are provided. Guests do the singing, solo or in groups. Food and beverages are part of the package. Often souvenir T-shirts are included.

Theme Restaurants like an Automat or '50s diner can be a fun setting for a kids' party. Some will include music, others will not.

Museums sometimes have party facilities. Not that the Metropolitan Museum of Art is the right venue for a Bar/Bat Mitzvah party, but children's museums may be. In Boston, the Children's Museum and the Computer Museum have both hosted Bar/Bat Mitzvah parties.

You will get other ideas by keeping your eyes open, watching for advertisements in newspapers and magazines, and just generally asking around.

Handling a Bar/Bat Mitzvah When Parents Are Divorced

Bar and Bat Mitzvahs are among those life-cycle events that touch us very profoundly. They can kick off a slew of emotional issues in the best of circumstances and within the most tight-knit of families. When there's been a divorce, the situation immediately gets more complicated.

Whether or not the day is successful depends not so much on how amicable or bitter the divorce was but on how the parents have learned to co-parent since the breakup. If new relationships have been established around the child, putting the child's best interests first, then it's likely the Bar/Bat Mitzvah day will go smoothly and be fulfilling for everyone. If not, the child's big day will probably be just one more battlefield.

But no matter how acrimonious their feelings toward each

other, there is one thing divorced couples can usually agree on: their love for and pride in their child and the desire to make the day a peaceful one for him or her. By focusing on the child, some couples are able to bury the hatchet, at least temporarily. Of course, that's easier said than done, but it's important to remember that no matter how difficult the situation may be for you and your ex, it's harder still on the child.

In a divorce situation, it's more crucial than ever to discuss things beforehand, through a third party if necessary. If certain things can be ironed out up front, there's a better than average chance of success. You could start by writing down all the issues that might come up and think about which you are willing to compromise on and which you aren't.

In terms of the service itself, issues that need to be dealt with include aliyot (his side, your side, etc.); who will be involved if there's a passing-down-of-the-Torah ritual; and who will make a parent's prayer or speech. Obviously, the ideal situation would be for both parents to work together in planning the day, but that's not always going to be possible. Hopefully, finding some common ground will be.

You also will want to think about how the invitations will read, if they will be from the Bar/Bat Mitzvah child, and where your name and that of your spouse will appear.

If either of you has remarried, what part will the new spouse play in the proceedings? Will his or her family be involved and to what extent?

In terms of the reception, you will need to decide on the format, and of course, how it will be paid for. In many cases where no agreement can be reached on this issue, divorced couples have opted for a children's-only party, or in some cases two receptions, one held by the mother for her family and friends and the other hosted by the father. If that's the arrangement you end up with, try not to have both parties take place on the same day. That would be hard on the child—whose occasion it is supposed to be.

Talking with your child's rabbi is always a good idea whether or not you run into problems. After all, rabbis have dealt with this specific situation before and may be able to offer up workable ideas. Going for professional counseling is another possibility. Best of all, however, may simply be talking to people who have gone through it. If you don't know anyone, chances are the rabbi does. By listening to the solutions reached by others, you may very well find a perfect one for your situation, and end up with a Bar/Bat Mitzvah that makes everyone happy.

Chapter Seventeen

Why Not Chuck It All and Go to Israel?

The idea of a child becoming a Bar/Bat Mitzvah in Israel holds a powerful attraction for reasons spiritual, familial, and practical. Marking one's coming of age in the Jewish homeland provides an emotional tie to our people. When a child walks the streets in the city of Solomon, near where Abraham and Sarah are buried and where David sat by the stream, the isolated incidents learned about in Hebrew school become living history. There is no way the Bar/Bat Mitzvah could be perceived by your child as just a big party. The impact can be so powerful, it could mark a turning point in the child's Jewish commitment. Indeed, having your child's celebration in Israel could be looked at as an investment in our future as a people, an insurance policy for Jewish survival. At the very least, it should strengthen the link between American Jews and Israelis and boost tourism there.

If you have family in Israel, the pull becomes even more powerful. What could be more joyous than bringing together relatives who live far apart on this most important day in your child's life? A Bar/Bat Mitzvah in Israel may also resolve potential problems for families in which there has been a divorce. There is much less to deal with in terms of "his side or her side," all the way down the line, from the ceremony to the celebration.

From a financial standpoint, the reasons are no less compelling. Working out the figures, you may very well find that for the same money spent for a hundred and fifty people at a catering hall for five hours, you can take twenty close family and friends to Israel for a week, all expenses included!

The reality is that many people choose Israel their second or third go-round on the Bar/Bat Mitzvah circuit. They have already gone the route of two hundred of their nearest and dearest whooping it up at the Hilton, and perhaps found that it didn't satisfy on a spiritual, deeply emotional level. Going to Israel seems more meaningful, for themselves and most certainly for the child.

The first decision to make is where in Israel to go. Although most Americans who go there choose to have the ceremony at either the Western Wall in Jerusalem or atop the ruins at Massada, the truth is with enough advance planning and research, you can see your child become a Bar/Bat Mitzvah in a synagogue or at a historical site. Here are some suggestions, plus the pros and cons of each.

The Western Wall

Perhaps the most famous site in the entire country, the Western Wall, is all that remains of the original Temple in Jerusalem. It is also called the Kotel. Bar Mitzvah ceremonies are routinely held there. They are public, and often many are going on at the same time. It can be very congested. The ceremony is Orthodox and only boys may read from the Torah. While you may have a Bat Mitzvah there, a male—her father, usually—will do the Torah reading in her honor. Bar/Bat Mitzvahs at the Wall are held only on Mondays and Thursdays, or on festival days. They are also held very early in the morning, usually at six to eight o'clock. Often there are enough people there already to form a minyan, but sometimes you may have to bring your own, exclusive of women, since the ceremony is Orthodox. At the Wall, women are separated from men, and witness the ceremony from behind a waist-high partition. Their area is often extremely crowded with women from other families.

There is no charge for a Bar/Bat Mitzvah at the Wall, but donations are accepted. You must arrange for your own rabbi, however. You can do this through the Israel Government Tourist Office, but the rabbi will be Orthodox (Reform and Conservative rabbis are often reluctant to officiate at the Wall). And bring a Sefer Torah.

Massada

Massada is the ruins of the hilltop fortress above the Dead Sea, the last stronghold of Jewish revolt against the Romans, where defenders committed mass suicide rather than surrender. Massada is a dramatic symbol of freedom and hope. For American Conservative and Reform Jews, it has become an even more popular place than the Western Wall for Bar/Bat Mitzvahs.

The service at Massada takes place outdoors in one of the excavated rooms, either the Synagogue, or the Chamber of Scrolls. The drama of looking out across the desert and down at the Dead Sea is incomparable. On the other hand, in summer an outdoor service can be very hot.

The area your child will become a Bar/Bat Mitzvah in holds only twenty to thirty people. You must provide a rabbi and Sefer Torah (most tour packagers will do this for you) and although there is no set fee, a donation of a few hundred dollars is fairly standard. At Massada, the Bar and Bat Mitzvah ceremonies are the same; your daughter may read from the Torah and there is no separation of men and women guests.

Like the Wall, however, Massada is not private. There may be more than one ceremony going on at the same time, and busloads of tourists will be peeking into your ceremony. Bar/Bat Mitzvahs are routinely held on Mondays and Thursdays as well as Saturdays, but like the Wall, extra early, due to the heat factor. Cable cars run up to the summit, but even then, the walk is significant. There is a charge for the cable cars. Fall and winter are preferable to summer Bar/Bat Mitzvahs (again, because of the heat and the crowds). Thanksgiving and Presidents' Week in February are ideal dates because they are holidays in the States and people can get away for a few days.

Israeli Synagogues

You may choose to have your Bar/Bat Mitzvah in an Israeli synagogue. With enough advance notice and planning, most will be able to accommodate you. A popular choice for a Reform service is Congregation Hal El in Jerusalem. They have extensive experience in working with American families. But you can find other Reform congregations by contacting the Association of Reform Zionists of America (ARZA), at 838 Fifth Avenue, New York, NY 10021. To get information on a Conservative congregation in Israel, write to Moreshet Israel, 4 Agron Street, P.O. Box 7456, Jerusalem 91073, Israel. The Center for Conservative Judaism in Jerusalem is another source.

Hadassah Hebrew University Medical Center Synagogue

Especially for Bat Mitzvahs, this is becoming a popular choice. The synagogue represents the tradition of strong Jewish women and reflects the values and goals of Hadassah. The service, however, is Orthodox, and girls do not read from the Torah, only the haftarah. The rabbi comes with the package, which for several hundred dollars includes the use of the synagogue for two hours, during which is it closed to outsiders.

Other popular places include the Hebrew Union College in Jerusalem (if you're not connected to it, however, or know someone who is, it's only available on Shabbat afternoon, or Mondays and Thursdays); the Peace Forest outside Jerusalem; the World Union of Progressive Judaism Youth Hostel, Beit

Shmuel; the slopes of Mount Scopus; or the steps at the Southern Wall.

Getting Information

If Israel is on your agenda, you would do well to start your research two years ahead of time. It may take awhile for you to gather all the information you need to make the decision that works best for your family. Know first that in order for your child to become a Bar/Bat Mitzvah there, boys must be thirteen years old plus one day according to the Hebrew calendar and girls twelve and one day. Know also that you do not need to forego the reception, including kiddush, music, photos, and videos. All these can easily be set up for you in Israel.

A good place to start gathering nitty-gritty details is by writing to the ARZA. They put out a pamphlet with suggestions. Their address was given above, or call them at (212) 249-0100. To contact Congregation Hal El, also mentioned above, write to the Israeli Movement for Progressive Judaism, 13 King David Street, Jerusalem 94101, Israel.

Working through the Israel Government Tourist Office is another popular method of divining your options. They have six locations in the United States and one in Canada. Write (or call) the one closest to you. In New York, 350 Fifth Ave., 19th Floor, New York, NY 10110, (212)-560-0650; in Chicago, 5 South Wabash Ave., Chicago, IL 60603, (312)-782-4306; in Los Angeles, 6380 Wilshire Blvd., Los Angeles, CA 90048, (213)-658-7462; in San Francisco, 220 Montgomery Street, Suite 550, San Francisco, CA 94104, (415)-775-5462; in Miami, 420 Lincoln Road, Suite 326, Miami Beach, FL 33139, (305)-673-6862; in Washington, D.C., 3514 International Drive NW, Washington, DC 20008, (202)-364-5500; and in Canada, 180 Bloor Street West, Suite 700, Toronto, ON M5S 2V6 (416)-964-3784.

Aside from giving you the information you need, the Israel Government Tourist Office will mail you a card to fill out and submit directly to the offices either for the Western Wall or for Massada about two months before your requested date. They provide a rabbi at the Wall, but not at Massada.

The Hadassah Travel Department, at 50 W. 58th Street, New York, NY 10019, is another source, or you could write directly to the Hadassah Medical Organization in Jerusalem, P.O. Box 12000, Jerusalem 91120, Israel.

Many *travel agents* and *tour operators* are adept at setting up Bar/Bat Mitzvahs in Israel. Indeed, many offer all-inclusive packages. The attraction is that they do all the setting up for you. On the other hand, everything including the site is chosen by the tour operator (and most chose Massada). A typical Bar/Bat Mitzvah package set up by a tour operator or travel agent will include morning services with a kiddush, an Israeli rabbi to conduct the service, a group reception (these package deals are usually done with a tour group, so others will be getting at the same time), and some commemorative gifts. Each package has its own extras thrown in, so comparison shopping is worthwhile. Some packages offer free air fare for the Bar/Bat Mitzvah child, and most include a tour of Israel on the itinerary.

If you want to use a travel agent, but prefer to have a customized itinerary, and not be part of a group, you must state that strongly at the outset. Not every travel agent will be willing to cooperate, so it is imperative to shop around.

When working with a travel agent, know exactly what you want. Draw up a list of questions ahead of time. Assume nothing, and ask about everything, from who the rabbi they provide will be, what the rabbi actually does (one woman was upset when the rabbi at Massada left immediately after the service and didn't even share wine and challah with the family) to what the package includes. If you want a car, say so. And make sure everything is written up to your satisfaction.

A few reputable tour operators: ITAS (Israel Travel Advisory Service), 18 Canoe Brook Drive, Livingston, NJ 07039, (201)-992-5073 or (800)-326-ITAS. Also Margaret Morse

Tours, Inc., 17070 Collins Ave., Suite 262, Miami Beach, FL 33160; and Ayelet Travel, Ltd., 21 Aviation Road, Albany, NY 12205, (518)-437-0695 or (800)-237-1617. Looking in Jewish newspapers or magazines is a good way to find tour operators and travel agents in your area.

More Tips

- When choosing a tour operator or wholesaler, it's a good idea to find one with a branch in Israel, just in case something goes wrong while you're there.
- Learning as much as you can about Israel before you go will enhance the trip immeasurably.
- Fall and spring are the best times of year to go.
- Think about taking out cancellation insurance, just in case!
- Buy State of Israel bonds to take with you.
- It is customary at the Wall for people to throw small hard candies at the Bar/Bat Mitzvah. The gesture symbolizes the sweetness of the occasion. So don't be surprised by the pelting, or the hordes of children looking to pick up the candy.
- Before you make any decision, *talk to others who have done this before.* The only way to really find out the pros and cons is through someone with experience who is not trying to sell you anything. Be sure to ask what, if any, the negatives were. The more information you factor in, the better your chances of a successful, fulfilling trip.

Does Your Child Want to Go?

Most youngsters do, but even those who are most eager have mixed feelings. What about all the friends back home? It's normal for your children to want to include all their friends at the Bar/Bat Mitzvah, something that is obviously impossible in Israel. That is why many who chose Israel end up having a second reception back home for the child's friends. Along those lines, you may also want to think seriously about the people close to you. Can you really just pick twenty or thirty and leave out the rest? It may be very difficult and you may find yourself responsible for two affairs. And if your child has a relationship and rapport with the rabbi at your temple, how will he or you feel about not having that rabbi officiate? The decision is very personal, but before you make it, consider all the angles. It may turn out to be a unique occasion and a wonderful trip besides.

Chapter Eighteen

What Can Go Wrong...

...usually doesn't, but it's perfectly normal to worry about it anyway. (Worrying comes with the territory of being a Jewish mother, or didn't you know that by now?) When it comes to your child's Bar/Bat Mitzvah there are two kinds of worries: the what-ifs, terrible things you imagine in your waking hours, and the Mitzvahmares, the kind that come to you in your sleep and from which you wake up at three A.M. in a cold sweat. Just in case you haven't experienced this part of the Bar/Bat Mitzvah planning yet, here's a bit of what you are in for, based on the true confessions of myself and others. By the time you have had your own Bar/Bat Mitzvah, no doubt you will be able to add to this list substantially.

What If...

- Your child blanks out on the bimah, freezes and forgets every word of Hebrew? (There is a way to prevent this. You can buy him/her a Bar/Bat Mitzvah "Protector": see Chapter 21.)
- The child is so nervous he or she throws up on the bimah? (No breakfast that day!)
- He or she is nervous and laughs, cries, or has the hiccups in the middle of the haftarah?

- He or she loses a contact lens and can't read anything?
- Feuding family members start a loud argument during the service?
- Great-uncle Burt falls asleep and snores so loudly everyone starts to laugh?
- Someone brings a baby that starts to cry during the service, and the parents don't walk out?
- A toddler runs up and down the aisles and creates a disturbance while your child is reciting the prayers?
- You fall or trip going up to the bimah?
- The heat or air conditioning doesn't work at the temple/reception?
- There's a terrible snowstorm and everyone cancels?
- The Bar/Bat Mitzvah child wakes up with chicken pox that morning?
- There's a death or serious illness in the family?
- The directions you sent are wrong and everyone gets lost?
- You made the food and it burned?
- The food comes out underdone, or cold?
- There's not enough food?
- Everyone gets food poisoning?
- At your low-key buffet, people are three deep on line and not happy about it?
- The bartender serves drinks to underaged kids?
- The band or deejay doesn't show up (this is my all-time favorite)?
- The band or deejay does show, but plays terrible music and no one dances?
- Everyone dances, but the dance floor's too small?
- Someone leans over to light a candle and her hair catches on fire?
- The place you've booked goes out of business three weeks before the affair?

Do some of these sound familiar? Others completely ridiculous? Guess what? Most of them have happened. And guess what else? Every situation was dealt with, and solved.

Now for the even more irrational fears, these things have not happened, to my knowledge, but that doesn't mean you won't dream about them.

Mitzvahmares:

"I dreamt that the alarm didn't go off and we all overslept."

"I dreamt that people came to the house early and I wasn't ready; my hair wasn't done and I didn't know my prayers yet."

"I dreamt that we were at the reception, but in the wrong clothes. And I thought, Where are all the beautiful clothes I bought? Why are we in these schmattes?"

"My daughter dreamt that all the guests showed up in bunny costumes. When she asked me why, I told her that was our theme, bunnies. She was very upset."

"I dreamt that we were all on a bus, all the family, friends and even the rabbi, going to our son's Bar Mitzvah. And I suddenly realized that he had never studied, and didn't know a thing."

"I dreamt that none of the guests showed up."

"I dreamt that a huge number of people we didn't invite showed up and crashed the party."

"I dreamt that we had a swim party and not one person went in the water."

"I dreamt that I looked around and it was all someone else's family at the service, not ours."

"I dreamt that there was a world catastrophe and we couldn't have the Bar Mitzvah!"

Chapter Nineteen

Survival Strategies: Tips from A to Z

When choosing ACCOMMODATIONS for out-of-town guests, ask if the hotel will transport them to the temple. Many hotels will do so, either as a service or for a very nominal fee. This avoids out-of-towners getting lost and your worrying that they won't arrive in time for the ceremony.

Before the situation arises, decide how you feel about BABIES, at the service and/or reception. Even when you have not invited them, chances are you will receive at least one frantic phone call from a young mother explaining that she cannot get a baby-sitter, may she bring the baby to the Bar Mitzvah? Otherwise, she can't come. If you would really prefer not to have the distraction of an infant or toddler (after all, one presumes you did not invite them for a reason), offer to provide an experienced baby-sitter in your home—at your expense. That way, mother and child are never too far apart, mother can check in with child as often as she wants, and you have been a gracious host. If the parents decide not to accept your offer and end up declining your invitation, don't feel bad; you did extend yourself and it was their decision not to come.

COORDINATE all timing with the appropriate people. This is especially necessary when everyone will be heading straight to the reception from the temple. First find out when the service ends. After building in time for schmoozing (and getting coats if

162

the season warrants) and traveling to the party place, tell the caterer when the first guests can be expected (err on the early side, just in case). You should also tell the band or deejay, florist/balloon people, photographer/video person, and anyone else expected to participate in your reception. Notify everyone in writing and with a follow-up phone call. Also, coordinate "caravans" if you think there is a chance guests unfamiliar with the neighborhood will flounder, in spite of your fabulous directions. Ask friends to head up the caravans and tell relatives which friends to follow.

DRESS as in "the Dress" and "dress requirements": More people seem to get bent out of shape (could it be because they perceive themselves as being perennially out of shape?) about what they are going to wear than any other part of the whole megillah. Indeed, many people focus all their pre–Bar/Bat Mitzvah anxiety right there. Some tips, then, to take the edge off:

For you: Shop early and shop often. Do not—repeat, do not— leave it until the last minute, no matter how much of a trauma it is. It may take quite a while to find what you want. It may have to be ordered. It almost certainly will have to be altered. Extra angst about whether the dress will be ready on time is seriously unnecessary. Besides, you will need time with the dress in hand to choose shoes, stockings, jewelry, and other accessories.

Cruise boutiques, bridal shops (no, silly, for *mother*-of-the-bride dresses), off-price stores, and department stores. Don't rule anything out. You never know.

Don't rule out suits. Some are just breathtaking and most are more flattering to your figure.

In custom shops, ask about dresses in sample sizes. Usually they are 8s and 10s, and often available for a fraction of the price.

In terms of color, there are no rules, except you might want to be careful about white (because, you don't need the extra worry).

The *money* thing: there are really two ways to go into this. One is the sentimental: "I'm prepared to spend a lot more than I normally would on a dress, because this is a once-in-a-lifetime occasion and I don't care if I never wear it again. Besides, it will be immortalized for posterity in the pictures." Or the practical: "No way will I spend a lot of money on something that will sit in the closet. Of course I'll wear it again and I'm not going into hock over this dress." Neither rationale is right or wrong. Do what's right for you.

No matter what you spend, the dress you purchase should make you feel special. If you think you look great, you will be calmer about other things that day.

That said, the dress still must be *comfortable*. Try it on in various situations before purchase or final alterations. You should be able to *move* in it, *sit* in it (without its riding up), and go to the *bathroom* in it without having to take it off. Disasters I have seen or experienced include an exquisite leather outfit that was so tight (the mother of the Bat Mitzvah did have the figure for it) that the skirt ripped right up the back during an especially active dance number. Then there was the straight leather dress with a silhouette so narrow that only after it was too late did the woman realize she could not pull it up over her hips to go to the bathroom (she suffered during the entire reception). And once my own skirt was so narrow around the knees that I could barely walk up the steps to the bimah (forget about getting in and out of a car) and, more embarrassing, the front snaps on the top unsnapped during every dance. (I had to get an unchic safety pin to hold myself together.)

Buy and bring with you several pairs of *extra stockings*. If you do not, it's a given, you will rip yours. If you have extra pairs on hand, you will be less nervous. You can always return the unopened ones.

Bring *socks* to the reception if you plan to dance. The kids always know to do this, but it is the adults in high heels who really need them. Kick off your heels, put on the socks, and dance the night away. It will save seriously sore feet in the morning. With this in mind, a friend found polka dot socks for me, to match the polka dots on my dress.

About *shoes:* unless you are really used to wearing high heels, it's probably a bad idea to wear them on this occasion. You will be nervous enough; do you really want to worry about tripping?

For the Bat Mitzvah girl: Again, start looking early. And if you live in an area boasting lots of expensive teen boutiques, you might want to go without your daughter first, to eliminate, if necessary, those that are just too prohibitive.

Remember—no, I take it back, you won't have to remember, because you will constantly be reminded—it's *her* day, and she will want to look really special. Once you have established the price boundaries, let her have free reign over her dress. She needs to feel comfortable and beautiful; she will be in the spotlight and anything that makes her feel calmer and more confident is worthwhile in the long run. Even if it is all sequined, or festooned with ribbons and bows.

That said, you can still guide her gently and let her know your feelings. I have a real problem with black on a Bat Mitzvah and my daughter knew it. She also knew, however, that aside from that, she pretty much could pick whatever she wanted. She was reasonable enough not to even look at anything black. I had to give in on the sequins. (Which, you should know, are almost impossible to clean; it was easier to buy extra sequins and sew them on top of the ones she dripped chocolate ice cream on.)

Don't rule out department stores. Sometimes you can do very well and find just the thing for a great price.

Address immediately the issue of whether she will ever wear the dress again and decide how you both feel about it. In truth, she has a better shot at wearing hers again than you do: she will probably have lots more Bar/Bat Mitzvahs to attend.

Buying extra stockings, and of course bringing socks to dance in, apply to her as well as to you.

For the Bar Mitzvah boy: Most of the boys are not quite as concerned about what they are going to wear. They know it will be a suit, and most likely a new one. Still, because suits do need to be altered and shirts and ties found to match, I wouldn't leave it to the last minute either. Check out department stores and boys' and men's clothing stores for colors, styles, and sizes and availability of sales help. This is one time you will need it.

Ask about alteration policies. Some upscale stores offer free alterations for a full *year* from the date of purchase. And since your son will most definitely grow, and you will want him to wear the suit again, this courtesy is a great money saver.

For the father: The dad of the Bar/Bat Mitzvah is probably the easiest person to outfit on this special day, for as one person noted, "Who would know if Russ's suit was even new or not?" Many men *want* to get a snazzy new suit for this occasion, and in that case they should. But if they have an extensive suit wardrobe already and they don't really care all that much, a hot new tie could do the trick nicely and save a few hundred dollars.

Dress requirements for Temple vary. In many congregations, improper dress is overtly frowned upon. It's a house of worship, after all, not a ballroom. In some temples, there are specific dress requirements that you must conform to in order to participate in the service. In others, the standards are alluded to but not formalized.

Your own sense of propriety is really what dictates, but here are some general tips: No bare shoulders on the bimah. Cover the cleavage and change into the miniskirt after you leave the sanctuary. In fact, if time allows, you might wear a more modest outfit to the temple and change completely for the reception. Or get an outfit with a matching jacket to wear during the service and take off at the reception.

Some dress shops may be able to help. The dress I wore to my daughter's Bat Mitzvah was basically bare-shouldered. The seamstress at the store used some extra material to devise what I called "bimah straps" that snapped in and covered my shoulders. Once the party began, I simply unsnapped them and stashed them in my bag.

EXERCISE is an important element, whether you think you are overweight or not. My own personal "Mitzvahmares" included a barely audible ripple running through the congregation as I

ascended the bimah: "Pssst... she's gained weight... pass it on
... she was thinner for her son's... couldn't she lose a few
pounds for her daughter's sake?" I also envisioned the song being
played when I came up to light a candle as the theme from *Mr.
Ed*—"A horse is a horse, of course, of course..." Okay, I do take
it to extremes, at least in my head, but regular exercise can
stave off the crazies: After a good workout, you'll be too tired to
worry.

I don't know about you, but I need a reason to exercise and a
Bar/Bat Mitzvah is a good one. So about a year before the big
event I started what I called the "Bat Mitzvah Trot." I began a
daily walking regimen of two miles per day, as fast as possible,
alone or in the company of a friend who also had a Bat Mitzvah
coming up.

FRIENDS who are there to support you, commiserate with you,
and help out with ideas and chores will never seem so cherished
as they do at this point in your life. Make time to be with your
friends, the emotional benefits are infinite.

Bring a small shopping bag to the reception to put *gifts* in.
People will be showering you with envelopes, your Bar/Bat
Mitzvah will be running up to you with gifts, and after a short
while *you'll* run out of places to stash them. Maybe you will
need a *big* shopping bag. Either way, placing it under the table at
your seat is one possibility. Many caterers will also put empty
bags aside for you.

One of the main things your child may be nervous about is
the HAFTARAH. You can help by coaxing him or her to chant it
out loud in your presence many times, and by your constant
reassurance that it really doesn't matter if they mess up. No one
will notice and you will still love them and think they are
terrific, no matter what.

INSIST, no matter how hard it is, that no one besides the
immediate family sleep over at your house the night before. No
grandmas, aunts, uncles, cousins, or friends from far away. You
do not need to be playing host; your child does not need the
distraction. Put them up with friends, or at a nearby hotel.

JUXTAPOSE baby and growing-up pictures of all the children

and as many of the adult guests as you can with a meaningful poem ("Forever Young") and create a collage to put next to the sign-in board. Everyone looks for themselves: a great icebreaker.

KEEP EVERYTHING, every phone number, every bill, every lead, every scrap of information relating to the event. Make a Bar/Bat Mitzvah file and save it to pass around to friends. There is really no reason everyone has to start from scratch.

LAUGHTER AND LISTS will help keep you sane. Laughter, lots of it, is the best antidote for Bar/Bat Mitzvah jitters. See comedies, pick books from the Humor section, get together with friends. Make lists, many of them, and revise them daily. As you check things off, you will feel empowered. Make a list of all the things you are worried about that you have no control over. Then tear it up.

Ask an elderly relative to do the MOTZI (prayer) over the challah. He or she will be especially honored.

NETWORK. Can't find a suitable place in your neighborhood to hold the Bar/Bat Mitzvah? Don't know a good band? Your best bet always is asking around. Somebody will know somebody else, who will know exactly what you need to know.

ORGANIZE! Start with a loose-leaf binder with dividers and make sections for each category: guest list, caterer, music, decorations, aliyot, etc. Then put all related information into its appropriate section. Or use manila folders for each category and keep them all together within a bigger cardboard file folder.

Try to keep everything in PERSPECTIVE and not let the preparations become all-consuming. People who make this the only priority in their lives tend to lose perspective easily, and that is when the smallest mishap seems insurmountable. This is your child's birthday; it not only has religious significance but marks the passage from childhood to adolescence. If that isn't a sobering thought, I don't know what is. Now is the time, experts tell us, to be more attuned to what is going on inside your child's head than to worry about food and balloons. Still, the tendency to let this topic monopolize all your conversations will turn you into a crashing bore. (I know: I'm guilty of this one.)

QUIT your job two weeks before the ceremony. I'm only kidding! But that is going to be the most intense time, when all the last-minute details have to be attended to. So if you have vacation time coming, this wouldn't be a bad time to take it.

Delegate RESPONSIBILITIES. Whatever doesn't have to be done by you personally can be handed over to someone else, provided they are willing, of course. You don't have to do it all yourself, and shouldn't, and—take it from someone who always thinks she can—you can't.

STRESS comes with the territory. Going in knowing you will be stressed out at times will help you deal with it. It helps, too, to realize that some things are beyond your control (the weather, people who get sick, the quality of the food, what songs the deejay really plays, if your child forgets the entire haftarah), so there is absolutely no point in worrying about them. *Everything will be fine.*

When you need to TRANSPORT children from the temple to the reception, and don't want to ask their parents to make the extra trip, there are basically two methods. One the kids will love, and will cost you. The second the kids won't love, but won't cost you anything except a little organization.

The first: call a local school bus company and rent the bus and driver. Arrange to have the bus waiting outside the temple after services and give them directions to the reception. Needless to say, kids love this, especially when there's no adult on board.

The second: when all the RSVPs are in, send postcards to adults who will have room in their cars saying, "You will be driving Lynn Mandelbaum, Carrie Gardner, and Michelle Eichler from the temple to the Sheraton. Meet them in the temple lobby at the conclusion of the service." Even if the adults don't know the kids, they will find them.

Concurrently, send postcards to the three children, telling them (and advising their parents at the same time) that "You will be driven from the service to the reception by Mr. and Mrs. Lautz. Please have your parents pick you up at the Sheraton at 5:30 P.M." That way, the kids are accounted for and it eliminates guesswork as well as twenty phone calls from parents asking what they should do.

When dealing with a caterer the very last week, UNDERESTI-MATE (by two or three couples) the number of guests you expect and *must* pay for. Caterers usually give you a deadline of two or three days prior to the party when you have to give them an exact number, and pay for that many. If fewer people show up—trust me, you will have last-minute cancellations—you are not stuck paying for no-shows. Don't be sneaky; tell the caterer you are doing this and you will be glad to pay extra if you have miscalculated. Most caterers are not only happy with this arrangement, but actually suggest it themselves. Advise them, of course, of the seating and place settings as if everyone were coming, but just pay for fewer.

VOTIVE CANDLES are pretty table decorations. Just don't put them on the dais. The kids will get into them and if you haven't worried about a fire beforehand, you don't want to start now.

In fact, WORRYING about what can go wrong is really a waste of time. After you've organized and done everything possible for a smooth day, let go. Most of the time nothing goes wrong, or what does is easily fixed. And as the oft-repeated phrase goes, if something does go wrong, no one will know but you. Examples abound: Entering the sanctuary, the grandfather of the Bat Mitzvah told his son, "I can't do my aliyah. I'm too nervous." Quickly, the son employed a backup (someone who knew the blessings) and when the grandfather's name was called, the backup ascended the bimah instead. No one knew the difference.

The Bat Mitzvah girl was too nervous to do her candle-lighting ceremony when she was scheduled to. The deejay kept the music going, people danced, started their dinners, and had a grand old time until several hours later when the girl was calmer. She did it then, and beautifully. If people realized the candle lighting (and attendant hora) were being held later than usual, no one really cared.

Upon entering the reception room with all their guests, the

host family realized too late that the room was woefully small for their group. "It became a much more intimate affair," they concluded, and one of the most memorable ever.

The Bar Mitzvah was scheduled for January and a major snowstorm hit the night before. No one was going to be able to come. The rabbi was willing to reschedule for later in the day, a Havdalah service. The caterer called up every single one of the guests and told them of the change. Everyone showed up and had a wonderful evening, eating the bagels and lox that had been prepared for brunch!

What's the worst that could happen? The child comes down with mononucleosis three months before the ceremony (it happened to us) and you have to postpone it. A close relative dies and you have to cancel or postpone. You have no control over any of this.

Facing your worst-case scenario and deciding on solutions really does help. File it away in the recesses of your brain and if you are lucky, it won't happen.

XEROX everything: every bit of correspondence between you and anyone you are working with; letters confirming what you have paid for (I usually xerox a copy of the check onto the letter); copies of the seating plan, the song list, the candle-lighting rhymes, parents' prayers, Torah blessings. I took copies of the last five things with me to the temple and reception *and* gave copies to friends to hold, just in case they were needed and my brain was in outer space. Wouldn't you know it, I ended up needing some of them. For example, the decorators forgot to put the socks (for dancing) on each table, but I had a xerox of how many pairs went on which tables and the caterer worked from that. Had my child misplaced the candle-lighting rhymes, we would have had a copy.

If the temple does not provide them or you want your own, order YARMULKES (kippot) six to eight weeks ahead of time. Get them through the temple's gift shop or sisterhood, any Judaica store, or catalogues such as *The Source for Everything Jewish* (their address may be found in Chapter 21). Many people personalize yarmulkes by having the child's name and the date of the occasion inscribed inside. Guests take them home as mementos, although some people feel a religious article is inappropriate as a souvenir. If you feel this way, use the temple's kippot.

A word about ordering your own. You can get them in many materials: silk, velvet, suede, leather, even hand-crocheted. The cost varies accordingly. And they *can* be custom-colored. When I walked into the neighborhood Judaica store, I blithely said I wanted six dozen yarmulkes in "Sea Foam." The salesman, hands on his hips, looked me straight in the eye and said, "Lady, Pinchas with the payess from Brooklyn, who's making your yarmulkes, doesn't know from sea foam. He knows from green." Pinchas was persuaded, however, with the help of a piece of perfect Sea Foam material, to make us yarmulkes to match. I thought they were pretty. Pinchas has also learned—in the New York area, anyway—to stitch them up in "Mets blue" instead of navy.

Finally, get plenty of ZZZZZ's the week before the big day. It may be hard because everyone is nervous and excited, but beauty rest will help you look and feel best for what will invariably end up being the best day of your life.

Chapter Twenty

The Big Day—and the "Afterbirth"

In a way, your child's Bar/Bat Mitzvah can be compared to giving birth. The gestation period is long, laborious, fraught with anxiety, and filled with hope and expectations. But on the Big Day, when the "baby" finally arrives, all the struggle and angst dissolves completely into the pure, magical, overwhelming joy of the moment.

The million little things you woke up in the night sweating about have not materialized, indeed, are no longer significant. On that day, you will not be concerned with how the food tastes or how many balloons are in each table bouquet. Those realities which seemed so pressing at one time will be replaced by another: the reality of the love and kindness and genuine warmth that surrounds you on this day.

When you see your child, standing tall and confident—even if his voice is breaking just a little—reciting the prayers, chanting the haftarah, the love and pride you feel toward that child will be all-consuming. You will see nothing else, you will hear nothing else; not the latecomers nor the rustling and whispering in the sanctuary. Every fiber of your being will be concentrated on that child and unconditional love for that child will wash over you, obliterating everything else.

And when you ascend the bimah and look down on the sea of shining faces of the friends and relatives who have come to be here with you on this day, your heart will soar. Indeed, you will glow with an inner peace and complete calm and fulfillment you didn't know you were capable of.

As you watch each person come up to light a candle on your child's cake, it will touch your soul in a place that during your daily, workaday world you rarely visit and sometimes even forget exists. When you see your friends out on the dance floor, holding hands and kicking up their heels in a celebratory hora, you will truly be on another plane altogether, flying high, completely immersed in the moment.

When you reflect on the genuine warmth and bonding of not only family and friends, but Jews the world over who celebrate this moment, the feeling is nothing if not deeply spiritual.

For the Big Day of your child's Bar/Bat Mitzvah is truly a magic day. It's a day when all the disagreements, arguments, petty jealousies, and negativity seem picayune, and are instantaneously forgiven and forgotten. The love, warmth, and generosity of spirit of those who envelop you is what will finally overwhelm you and what you will remember and carry with you.

And that's why, after the last *aleinu,* after the last dance is danced and the last bill is paid and the last guests have kissed you goodbye, that this day will rank right up there, deep in your soul, with your wedding day and the day your child was born, as one of the highlights, one of the best days of your life.

Yes, on one level it *is* over quickly, but on another, it lasts forever.

The Afterbirth

It is precisely because we want these warm feelings to go on forever—or for as long as we can stretch them—that many people have what my cousin Eileen Eichler calls an "afterbirth." The afterbirth is when you invite a small group of your closest friends and family home (or have an open house, if you desire) to basically hang out, watch the video, relax, and, even though everyone is so stuffed and couldn't possibly eat another thing, ever, eat again. It is also the time when the Bar/Bat Mitzvah invites his or her closest friends over (this time, I'd put a strict limit on the number of kids) so *they* can hang out, rehash the day, watch the video, and yes, eat again.

Afterbirths are generally held in the evening, if the reception has been a luncheon, or for brunch the next morning if you've had a nighttime affair. Either way, it is the perfect time to really sit down and visit with people you couldn't possibly devote time to during the ceremony or party.

It's the time when you strip off the finery—and who cares if you put a run in your stockings now?—kick off the high heels, slip into comfy socks, jeans, and T-shirt, let out a major sigh of relief that it's all over and went better than you ever dreamed it could, kick back and let it all hang out.

The fun part is watching the video over and over—it may very well be the only time you watch the video! Many videographers will hand it to you unedited at the end of the day so you can enjoy it, then take it back later for further editing. There is no way you can have absorbed all that went on at the party, so viewing the video allows you to experience all you missed and listen to what your guests said during their interviews, which is often funny and sometimes touching. Viewing it in the company of friends and relatives, who are after all "starring" in it, makes it even more fun.

The refreshments served at the afterbirth can be really simple, but should—like everything else—be planned for ahead of time. If you are catering the party, the easiest thing is to arrange for more food to be delivered to your house by the same caterer. Although some people get really involved and hire a caterer to be there and make omelets and crêpes, it need not be that fancy: bagels, deli, even leftovers from the party, plus coffee and bakery treats, all served in paper plates and hot cups, are just fine. And your guests will be glad to help themselves. You don't have to be the host anymore. The point of the afterbirth, in fact, is for everyone to tell you how wonderful it was and for you to realize that they are right. That it *was* the best Bar/Bat Mitzvah ever!

Chapter Twenty-One

Gifts and Thank-yous

Some years ago there was a popular play staged in New York entitled "Today I Am a Fountain Pen," spoofing the inevitable gift that Bar Mitzvahs traditionally received. We have come a long way. If that play was being written now, its title would probably be "Today I Am a Series EEE U.S. Savings Bond," or "Today I Am a Gift Certificate to the Gap."

The nature of Bar/Bat Mitzvah gift giving may have changed over the years, but the idea of giving something of lasting value still seems important to adults. Most will give your child a savings bond or a personal check. The gift certificates to the trendy store of the moment usually come from the child's friends and are most often given to Bat Mitzvahs, as is jewelry. This, naturally, tends to please the kids more than those checks or bonds do, which they often don't see until college rolls around.

There are, however, many other creative kinds of gifts to give, or to suggest should someone ask what the child would like, or what you would like for him or her. Here are some possibilities that underscore the religious significance of this special birthday gift.

- Prayerbooks, bibles, or books on Jewish history or traditions. Though many youngsters may not appreciate these

177

right now, they very well may be the start of a fine Jewish literary collection in later years.

- Books relating to Jews, but which are written on a more popular plane, such as *The Jewish Book of Why, Jews in Sports,* or any topic that the child can relate to.
- Books by famous Jewish authors such as Elie Weisel, Natan Sharansky, or Sholom Aleichem.
- *My Bar/Bat Mitzvah,* a personal album published by the Union of American Hebrew Congregations, in which the child fills in all information, from his or her Torah portion to a listing of all the guests.
- Ritual items such as a kiddush cup, tallit, Shabbat candlesticks, or Menorah. Once again, these may be cherished only in the future, but certainly are of lasting value.
- Jewelry such as a mezuzah or a chai for his/her bedroom doorway.
- A laminate of the child's Torah portion or haftarah, framed and ready to hang on the wall. Expensive, but what could be a more appropriate memento of the day?
- *State of Israel bonds* are as appropriate for this occasion as U.S. Savings Bonds are.
- Small brass sculptures of the Bar/Bat Mitzvah child reading from the Torah on a marble slab, with the child's name and the date engraved. These may be found in Judaica stores or catalogues and are made to order.
- "Bear Mitzvah," a pink or blue teddy bear wearing a tallit and kippah.
- Tickets to a Jewish play, concert, or event.
- Teen membership in the local YM-YWHA or JCC.
- A Bar/Bat Mitzvah "Protector," a small metal and stained-glass statuette of the child holding a prayerbook. Attached is a card that says, "Hello, Bat Mitzvah Girl (or Boy), I am your personal protector. I will protect you against shaky hands, a squeaky voice, stomach butterflies, and forgetting all the Hebrew you ever knew. I guarantee a super party, exchangeable gifts, and a permanent feeling of pride. Don't lose me!"

- A large, decorative box in which the Bar/Bat Mitzvah child may store all the memorabilia of the day.
- A framed copy of the invitation.
- A donation of tzedakah in the child's name.

You can find any of these gifts in Judaica stores, your temple's gift shop, or in Jewish catalogues such as *The Source for Everything Jewish,* Hamakor Judaica, Inc., P.O. Box 48836, Niles, IL 60648.

Saying Thank-you

Naturally, your child will be acknowledging all gifts received—though you may have to nag him or her a bit to do it. The easiest way to keep track of gifts is by using the same system you started when you invited your guests. Hopefully, you created columns to track the gifts and to check off as each is acknowledged. Handwritten lists, computer printouts, RSVP cards, or index cards are once again the easiest way.

If you have ordered note cards at the same time as the invitations, they will be in hand when you need them. If you have not, using store-bought plain note cards makes sense. It is customary to send thank-you notes within three to four weeks of the occasion. Suggest that your child do a few each day, which will make the task seem less overwhelming.

While some youngsters are very creative in expressing their thanks, many cannot come up with anything beyond the standard "Thank-you for your generous gift and for sharing my special day." There is nothing wrong with that, but you might want to encourage your kid to mention the specific gift if it was something besides money, such as, "Thank you so much for the mezuzah, I am wearing it now," or to a friend, "I'm glad we're friends. It meant a lot to me that you attended my Bar/Bat Mitzvah."

While sending thank-yous, you won't want to overlook the rabbi, cantor, teachers, and anyone else connected to the temple who helped make the day as glorious as it was. Along with a donation (it needn't be large; it really is the sentiment that counts here), a personal note is a nice and much appreciated touch, a fitting way to close the book on this momentous occasion.

Chapter Twenty-Two

Reflections

Through the pages of this book, I have intertwined my own opinions and experiences with those of many others. In this final chapter, I should like to give them the opportunity to share some thoughts and to reflect on the experience.

The Mothers

Our celebration was one of the most important days of our lives. It was a wonderful statement of our love for each other and for our lives. The best part was the coming together of all the people we love and who we believe have a fondness for us; the mutual adoration and caring was a real high. The fact that my brother—at age thirty-eight—had a heart attack precisely one week later (he is fine now) underlined the significance and frailty of the experience.
—Diane Klein

For my daughter, the memorabilia of the day was a very big thing. We have a box that we kept everything in, all the response cards, the temple announcement, the invitation, the program of the Friday night service, all that was meaningful. She also took the group photo of all the kids, all her friends, had it blown up to poster size, and put it over her bed. That was her idea. There's something very powerful and significant about that large group picture. It really indicates how much this was a part of her life, her next step into adulthood. It wasn't just a party. She took a lot of it with her.

—Jane Kalfus

I think it's a crazy ritual we Jews go through, that we put ourselves through, so we can impress our fellow Jews. Why? To show we've survived and prospered! To stand up and shout that we are still here! But it makes no logical sense. Why spend the equivalent of a full year's college tuition, when we Jews value education so highly? Why spend the equivalent of a down payment on a house when we Jews value property ownership so highly? Or spend the time commitment and family strife when we Jews value marital understanding so highly? I don't know. I don't know why *we* did this, when we knew it wasn't our style to throw such a showy party. Peer pressure, at our age? Probably. I wish I knew the answer, so I could justify in my own mind the price I paid.

Making a Bar Mitzvah is like spending $40,000 on a new Mercedes. You pay for the car, drive it out of the showroom, and for five hours you have the time of your life in that car. It rides perfectly, handles better than you ever could have imagined. You are so happy, so proud of yourself for owning and enjoying this fine car and for being able to afford it. You even hire a video man and photographer to record the event. You show yourself and the car off to all your friends, relatives, everyone you care about.

And then, after five hours are up, you drive it off a cliff!

—Eileen Eichler

The best part was that everyone enjoyed themselves and our daughter made us proud.

—Joyce Jaffe

I thought, How can I make these wonderful feelings continue? So I started going to Friday night services. Now, when I look up at that bimah, I see a little piece of my son's history up there. It's a beautiful feeling.

—Sandy Choron

The Fathers

While certain family issues must be taken into consideration, Bar and Bat Mitzvahs are primarily for the child to appreciate and enjoy. They should not be given just for the sake of having a party; we should not lose sight of the traditional significance. They should not be done to impress friends or family, but rather to share the occasion with them in a meaningful, comfortable way.

—Howard Jaffe

Bar/Bat Mitzvahs are narcissistic events, which have evolved as an unfortunate social norm within our socioeconomic group. While our Bat Mitzvah was wonderful, generating a bonding of family and close friends and offering a perspective on our personal lives and the evolution of our family, I was always cognizant of the absurd production. We enjoyed the creative opportunity it offered; we loved the personal challenge. But all this could have happened with far less show, far less expense—I know it!

—Russell Klein

The Bar and Bat Mitzvahs of my children were the first milestones that we passed in their growing up. It was an event that was traumatic in planning, but went smoothly. It was a great expense, but one of the happiest occasions I can recall. I have no regrets.

—Marvin Reisfeld

The actual service at the temple was more meaningful than the party. Carrie worked hard, showed poise, and did a beautiful job. I felt proud of her.

—Saul Gardner

Before the actual event, I just thought it was so much money for an overblown birthday party. But when I saw my daughter up there on the bimah, I felt so proud, I was kvelling. It was worth every nickel.

—Norman Goldberg

The Kids

It was important to me because I worked really hard and it made me feel I accomplished a lot.

—Sara Jaffe

I was very nervous. I was excited that I could do it. It was a very good feeling when I finished.

—Michelle Eichler

I was nervous and excited. But it was *great* when it was all over. I was surprised it was so easy.

—Mindy Eichler

The service was more meaningful, but the party was by far the best part.

—Carrie Gardner

After practicing and working so hard, the greatest feeling I ever had was when I finished my haftarah. There was a big grin on my face.

—Carrie Goldberg

The Author

No matter how religious or irreligious we consider ourselves, to most Jews, a Bar or Bat Mitzvah *is* a life-cycle event. It comes at the end of our kids' childhood chapter, the beginning of the teen years. It is a rite of passage, a milestone in our children's lives. It ranks right up there with their births, graduations, marriages. We look forward to and plan for it: it is a simcha.

Admittedly, as parents, we all come to this particular passage bearing our own personal, emotional baggage. Whether we even recognize it or not, the way we were brought up has a lot to do with the way we feel about our kids becoming a Bar/Bat Mitzvah.

My own family was neither religious nor learned. My brother became a Bar Mitzvah because, after all, that's what you did. No reason beyond that was needed. As a girl, though I was given the option of going to Hebrew school, I chose not to and that was accepted. When my own son was born, I wasn't even sure I cared much about his becoming a Bar Mitzvah.

My husband's family are concentration camp survivors. He and his brother were brought up in an Orthodox synagogue (Hebrew school five days a week) and of course became Bar Mitzvahs. Even though my husband is not particularly religious (although as he gets older, he seems to get more so) there was never any doubt—in *his* mind, anyway—that his children would become Bar and Bat Mitzvahs.

So, we came to this point in our lives from opposite directions. I still do not consider myself particularly pious and I still have my own mixed bag of emotions about religion in general. But I have no doubts at all that one of the most important things we have done for our children is to have them become Bar and Bat Mitzvah. For through this we have given them an identity with their heritage. By studying the religion they were born into, they have become a link in the chain. Our children know that they are *part* of something, of a people with a rich history and a tradition of which they can be proud.

By giving them (even if at times it was more like forcing upon them) a religious education, we have planted the seed. Our children now have a foundation to build whatever they chose in adulthood. Some seeds will grow sooner, some later, some maybe never at all. But as parents, by having them become Bar and Bat

Mitzvah, we have at least planted that seed and, in doing so, continued the tradition.

"I worried about a lot of things not falling into place, but they all did. The best part of the entire event was the service, that feeling of pride as we watched our daughter chant her portion, and the warmth that washed over us knowing we were sharing this time with so many friends and family. My advice: stay calm, relax, enjoy!"

—Karen Berchman

A Bar/Bat Mitzvah Timetable: What You Should Be Doing and When You Should Be Doing It

Don't panic. This timetable was devised based on areas with a heavy Jewish population where competition is keen for dates, catering halls, bands, and photographers. Even then, I have built in plenty of time. Chances are, in your area you may not need to do things quite as far in advance as I have indicated: adjust the timetable as applicable.

When the Child Is Born
Start saving! Only joking. But if you can, it's not a bad idea to start a "Bar Mitzvah club" savings account. If you don't use it, put it toward college.

Three Years Ahead of Time
Initiate discussions with your co-planner about the Bar/Bat Mitzvah itself and the format of the reception.
Get a date from the temple; or choose your own date.
Decide on the time of the service and reception.
Set a budget.

Two Years Ahead
Start looking for places to hold the reception.

187

Start investigating bands and deejays.

If a Bar/Bat Mitzvah in Israel is on your agenda, start making contacts and plans.

Make up a tentative guest list so you have a ballpark number of people you plan to invite.

Book the reception hall and/or caterer or make the decision to have the party at home or in temple or elsewhere.

Buy a loose-leaf binder with dividers, or start a filing system. Categorize and organize. Keep all business cards, estimates, notes, lists, etc. in their proper file.

One Year

Book the band/deejay.

Start looking around at possible decorations, florists, balloon people.

Start thinking about themes and color schemes.

Start looking around for a photographer/video person.

If it's to be a kids-only party, start the arrangements now.

Start a diet and exercise regimen.

Eight Months

Book the photographer and video person.

Chose the decorations/florist/balloon people.

Book any extra entertainment you plan to have.

Start looking for invitations.

Six Months

Order the invitations.

Start thinking about what kind of favors you want to give out.

Start learning the Torah blessings.

Expect "Mitzvahmares" to begin.

Four Months

Start work on any do-it-yourself projects you plan: center-pieces, collages, and the like.

Three Months
  Make up a final guest list.
  Order favors.
  Look for hotel possibilities for out-of-town guests.
  Order yarmulkes (kippot).
  Start shopping for clothes for the rest of the family.
  Start the Great Postage Stamp Hunt.
  Find a calligrapher.

Two Months
  Mail the invitations.
  Make up a song list.
  Make appointments with florist/balloon people to go over exactly what you want; they should make up samples now for your approval.

One Month
  Make hairdresser appointments.
  Go for final fittings of dresses, suits, etc.
  Purchase accessories: shoes, stockings, ties, shirts, socks, jewelry.

Two Weeks
  Book hotel rooms for out-of-town guests.
  Choose people for aliyot and honors—call and ask if they'd like to do it.
  Make up aliyot and honors "cue cards" and mail to appropriate people.
  Decide on people to come up for the candle-lighting ceremony and put them in order.
  Decide who will call the candle-lighters up and make up rhymes/introductions.
  Pick appropriate songs for candle-lighters.
  Send list of candle-lighters and songs to band leader or deejay.
  Send any other instructions to band leader/deejay: directions, reconfirming time.

Do seating charts of adults and kids.

Xerox seating charts and send to caterer.

Call people who haven't responded.

Decide who gets centerpieces and make up signs.

Order food for Oneg Shabbat.

Order food for Afterbirth.

Buy paper goods for Oneg and Afterbirth.

Buy coffee.

Meet with decorator/florist/balloon person to go over final table count, sign-in board, and anything else they will be handling.

Go to the rehearsal with your child.

Meet with the rabbi.

Write parents' prayer or speech.

Decide how the children will be transported to the reception: either hire a bus or devise car pools and advise appropriate people.

Send final instructions to photographer and video person, including lists of important people, driving directions, and timing.

One Week

Take formal family photos.

Coordinate all timing with everyone involved: caterer, band/deejay, etc.

Buy extra stockings.

Buy shopping bag for gifts.

Reconfirm everything with caterer.

Xerox copies of everything: prayers, speeches, room and table layout, candle-lighting rhymes; give to a friend to hold in case you forget anything you may need that day.

The Night Before

Get plenty of rest!

Prepare extra sets of driving directions to bring to temple with you.

That Day

Prepare to have the time of your life!

Expense Chart

Here's most of what you will be spending money on. Some items will not apply to your situation (consider yourself lucky!), but here's a way to start tracking those that do.

The Food

Luncheon	$_____
Dinner	$_____
Brunch	$_____
Kiddush	$_____
Oneg Shabbat	$_____
Afterbirth	$_____

The Caterer

Rentals: chairs, tables, linens, silver	$_____

The Party Place | $_____

Music

Band	$_____
Deejay	$_____
Prizes	$_____
Cocktail hour	$_____
Food for the band/deejay	$_____
Overtime	$_____
Props for games	$_____
Union fees, taxes	$_____

Extra Entertainment

Props/prizes for extra entertainment	$_____

Decorations

Flowers	$_____
Balloons	$_____
Sign-in board	$_____

Cocktail hour decorations $_____
Bimah flowers $_____
Roses for candle lighting $_____
Boudoir basket $_____

Favors

Kids' goody bags $_____
Adult goody bags $_____
Shopping bags $_____

Photographer

Base fee $_____
Extra fee for family portraits $_____
Album $_____
Proofs $_____
Grandparents' albums $_____
Feeding the photographer $_____

Video

Unedited $_____
Edited $_____
Extra copies $_____
Feeding videographer $_____

Invitations

Postage $_____
Calligraphy $_____
Thank-you notes and postage $_____
Directions cards and offsetting $_____
Napkins, matchbooks, etc. $_____
Seating cards $_____
Calligraphy on seating cards $_____

Clothing

Dress for you $_____
Dress/suit for Bar/Bat Mitzvah $_____
Suit for husband $_____
Outfits for siblings $_____
Shirts, ties $_____

Socks, stockings, shoes	$_____
Jewelry	$_____
Alterations	$_____
Hairdresser	$_____
Makeup	$_____
Cleaning bill	$_____

Hotel Rooms for Out-of-Towners	$_____
Transportation for Kids, Out-of-Towners	$_____
Postcards, stamps for arranging car pools	$_____
Baby-sitter	$_____
Yarmulkes	$_____

Trip to Israel

Air fares	$_____
Hotel	$_____
Food and expenses	$_____
Bar/Bat Mitzvah fee	$_____
Donations	$_____

Organizational Supplies

Loose-leaf binder, files, computer software, xeroxing	$_____

Gifts

Donations to temple, rabbi, cantor, etc.	$_____

Tips and Taxes

Waiters, bartenders, maîî ·e d', parking valet, custodian, coat check, rest room attendant, bus driver	$_____
Unexpected taxes	$_____
Tzedakah	$_____

Glossary

aliyah   The honor of being called to the Torah to recite a blessing; literally, "going up," or "to ascend." A section of the weekly Torah portion is also called an aliyah. Plural: *aliyot.*

Bar Mitzvah   "Son of the Commandments." A boy (of thirteen years and one day) who has reached religious majority; also, the ceremony marking the event.

Bat Mitzvah   "Daughter of the Commandments." A girl (of twelve years and one day) who has reached religious majority; a (sometimes parallel) ceremony marking the event.

bimah   In the temple or synagogue, the raised platform before the ark from which worship services are held.

b'rachot.   Blessings.

challah   Braided loaf of egg bread, traditional for Shabbat and holidays.

d'var Torah   A speech based on some portion of the Torah, explaining it.

haftarah   Readings from the biblical books of the Prophets. It is always read after the *Torah*   portion.

havdalah   The Saturday evening ceremony in which the congregation says goodbye to the Sabbath. It separates Shabbat from the rest of the week. Also performed at the end of major holidays.

havurah   Small private group.

hora   Traditional circle dance in which everyone joins.

kiddush   Blessing over the wine recited on Shabbat and on holidays; light refreshments served with the wine following a service.

kippah   Hebrew for skull cap, worn as sign of reverence for God; *yarmulke*   Plural: *kippot.*

kvell   Glow with pride and happiness.

194

maftir   The last section of the week's Torah portion.

meshuga   Nuts, crazy.

minyan   A prayer quorum of ten adult Jews.

mispocha   All the relatives.

mitzvah   Commandment, good deed. Plural: *mitzvot*.

motzi   Blessing over the bread recited before meals.

Oneg Shabbat   Friday or Saturday social gathering.

parasha   Weekly Torah portion read at services.

payess   Earlocks, worn by Orthodox Jewish males.

pitsela   Your child before his/her growth spurt.

Rosh Hodesh   First day of the month on the Hebrew calendar.

schmooze   Socialize.

seudat mitzvah   Festive celebration of a milestone; Hebrew for a
   commanded meal.

shonda   Shame.

sidra   Torah portion of the week, same as *parasha*.

simcha   Joy; a joyous celebration or party.

tallit   A four-cornered prayer shawl with specially tied fringes,
   worn at worship services.

tchatchke   Small, worthless object.

tefillin   Two black leather boxes, fastened to leather straps,
   containing portions from the Torah; also called phylacteries.

Torah   The scroll upon which are written the first five books
   of the Bible, the Five Books of Moses, the Jewish
   "Constitution."

tsuris   Grief.

tzedakah   Righteous giving, charity.

yarmulke   Yiddish for *kippah*.

Phrases You Will Be Hearing a Lot of (Sometimes, from Your Own Lips!)

"After all"—pregnant pause, during which you are presumably taking out your wallet—"it's *her* day/*his* day!"

"It goes by so quickly!"

"We're spending so much already—what's a few dollars more?"

"It takes on a life of its own!"

"You can't please everyone."

"So what if something goes wrong? No one will know but you."

About the Author

Randi Reisfeld is an editor, author, and a Jewish mother who has produced a Bar and a Bat Mitzvah and lived to tell (and write) about it!

Ms. Reisfeld is editorial director of 16 Magazine, a youth-oriented entertainment publication, and has written several books for teenagers. Among them biographies of actors *Johnny Depp* (St. Martin's Press), *The Stars of Beverly Hills, 90210,* (Bantam), *Luke Perry* (Bantam). And of singers—*Debbie Gibson* (Bantam) and *Matthew & Gunnar Nelson* (Bantam). She has also contributed to the autobiographies of *New Kids on the Block* (Bantam) and *Vanilla Ice* (Avon). Her book *So You Want to Be a Star* (Archway) is a guide for teenagers who want to break into show business.

Her articles have appeared in *The New York Times, Scholastic Magazine,* Welsh publications, and *Women's World.*

She is the current Bar/Bat Mitzvah chairperson at Temple Beth Or in New Jersey.